How To Turn Your Pain TO POWER

Depressed, Stressed and Stuck in a Rut? Discover 9 Biblical Secrets to Shift from Misery to Mastery and Live a Fulfilling Life.

BA (Hons) Pastoral Ministry

Foreword by Dr J.M. Thomas

DISCLAIMER

The names and identifying characteristics of certain individuals referenced in this publication have been changed. It is sold with the understanding that neither the author, nor the publisher is engaged in rendering any psychological or psychiatric help, or other professional advice. The strategies outlined within this book may not be suitable for every individual and are not guaranteed or warranted to produce your specific result. The author and publisher disclaim any responsibility for any liability, loss or risk, personal or otherwise, which is incurred as a consequence, directly or indirectly, in the use and application of any of the contents of this book.

COPYRIGHT

The paperback, e-book, and i-book editions were first published in 2013 by

Rose Chandler Companies.

© The estate of Rose Chandler 2013.

Rose Chandler has asserted her right to be identified as the author of this work in accordance with the Copyright, Designs and Patents Act 1988.

All rights reserved. No part of this publication may be reproduced, stored in a retrieval system or transmitted in any form or by any means, electronic, mechanical, photocopying, recording or otherwise, without the prior permission of the copyright owner.

All enquiries regarding performance, broadcasting or re-use of the material in this book should be addressed to the publisher.

A CIP catalogue record for this book is available from the British Library. Self-published by Rose Chandler Companies. Contact +447525-348007. RoseChandler.co.uk

Printed in the United Kingdom. ISBN - 978-1-907748-01-1

About the Author

Rose Chandler
Turn Around Expert, Accountant, Auditor and Christian Author

Rose Chandler is the CEO and Founder of Turn Around Consulting, Intelligent Services Ltd and Rose Chandler Foundation.

Rose is a Global Turn Around Expert who believes that every problem has a solution; it's a matter of perception. Everyday, Rose encounters people who have become stuck in life. They are stuck because of a past hurt, tragedy or a sequence of devastating events, which took a grip of their lives.

Rose understands their pain, because she was once stuck in life, taking two steps forward but one backwards. Rose was on the treadmill of life, moving but going nowhere, existing but not living. Rose came to the threshold of pain where she said "enough is enough." It was at the point of desperation that Rose started the search for strategies and tactics to address her thoughts, emotions and beliefs, when the personal turnaround of her life started. Rose researched and applied time tested Biblical strategies to turn around the pain of life threatening illness, sudden death in the family, redundancy, rejection, public humiliation to name a few. It was a process, it was not an overnight success, but Rose can proclaim that she has turned her pain into power.

This led Rose to write her first book on "How to Turn Your Pain into Power". In this book, Rose reveals a collection of timeless Biblical secrets. It gives a quick and easy access to anyone who is looking to smash through the pain of the past, so they can access their inner power for the future.

As a result of her own journey, Rose's passion is to empower people to find meaning in adverse situations and to make it work for their good. Rose loves to help people to understand that within them, are endless possibilities to build a successful and fulfilling life.

Rose is an accomplished author and public speaker with a successful track record in accounting, auditing and ministry. Rose has spent decades working with individual from all walks of life. When these individuals were exposed to the secrets in this book, they started a revolution in their own lives. They did the shift from misery to mastery and from pain to power.

Rose has had the privilege of working in Europe and the UK with her accounting and auditing profession, and now she is taking a dynamic message of personal power and hope to a hurting world. It's a message that will transform lives and minds to realise that everyone is valuable and priceless in the eyes of God.

Rose in committed to spread her message to a wider audience. As a result, Turn Around Consulting is committed to providing inspirational tapes, webinars, CDs, internet learning programs, workshops, workbooks, devotionals, coaching programs and memory joggers aimed at individuals who are committed to turning their lives around from pain to power.

Rose has turned her pain into power by writing and sharing the strategies that has helped her to survive and thrive. She has helped countless others to do the same. When you are ready for the remedy to your malady, feel free to email Rose on info@ RoseChandler.co.uk.

For the past thirteen years, Rose and her husband have been child sponsors to seven children who live in Africa and India. Rose has established the Rose Chandler Foundation, which, in collaboration with other like-minded charities, is committed to help to address:

- Homelessness in the UK
- Provision of education, clothing and nutrition to under-privileged children
- The supply of fresh running water to communities in Africa

You can track our progress on https://RoseChandler.co.uk

In Latin, the name Rose means one who transforms dreams into reality, one who is full of vigour and emotion, graceful in her approach and amazingly exciting. Should you meet Rose this is whom you will encounter. These qualities shine through in the book you are about to read.

In Praise of this Book

This is a profound and powerful book that is practical, and easy to read. If you are stuck in a rut, this is the book that will get you out if you follow the steps. I highly recommended this book to anyone who wants to turn his or her life around.

Elnette Parsons: Independent Mannatech Associate - UK
http://www.nutritioninanutshell.co.uk

What a breath of fresh air. This book is going to help so many people. It's practical and has so many truths on every page. I believe it's a must-read for every person, no matter what season of life they are in.

Shawn Basson: Assistant Pastor - South Africa
http://www.kingdomlightchurch.co.za

This is a compelling book. Rose has used her gift as an author to illustrate her life experiences. This has inspired me and helped me to understand and apply the nine simple steps to my life. I now have a robust plan for my life that is built around my purpose.

Marjorie Shepherd: Teacher - USA

Rose Chandler inspires you to take action and build the life you have always wanted. As you read this book, I am sure you will feel empowered and inspired to act. Her creation of the M.I.D.A.s™ tool and the D.E.S.I.R.E™ formula are life changing.

Kadia July: School Psychologist - Jamaica

How to Turn Your Pain to Power is packed with principles and techniques that will change your life forever when you apply them. Rose is a true expert on turn around principles. I will recommend this book to my friends and family.

Allison Taylor: Student - Canada

If you feel like you are stuck and must change, then you should read this book and put the principles in it to work. It's a powerful combination of encouragement and useful strategies to transform your life. You will return to this book again as you transition from pain to power.

Nadine Taylor
Attorney at Law - Jamaica

Acknowledgements

As I think of the many people I would like to thank for making this book possible the list continued to grow. First I would like to thank my Mom and Dad for their continuous love and support over the years. To my husband Martin who is supportive of my work and always has words of encouragement.

Thanks also to my Spiritual Father, Bishop J M Thomas who provided the foreword to this book and my Spiritual Mother, Mrs. J. Thomas.

My family has provided an environment for me to be expressive and creative. As a result I would like to thank my big sister Marjorie, and my big brothers Glen and Everton for always being present. I have to thank my cousin Nadine for her hard work to make my dream a reality. My niece Cheddeen was so supportive with her encouragement. To my much-loved aunts, uncles and relatives, who have remained strong in the face of many challenges.

Thank you to my friends Roger, Yvonne and Joseph and to my special friends and confidants. To the mothers and friends from the Globe Church and leaders and members of the Eagles Church for your support.

I thank God for His help, grace and mercy particularly during testing times in birthing this book.

Dedication

I dedicate this book to your success!

Be it.

Do it.

Love it.

Live it.

Contents

Foreword by: Dr. J. M. Thomas 13

Introduction 15

Section One: Turning on you - what's going on? 19

A, B, C - Admit, Beware, Compare 21

To Thine Own Self Be True 35

Section Two: Turning You Around – What Do You Want? .. 51

Born To Do What? 53

I Was Just Thinking 71

I Believe 87

Feeling Emotions 99

3-2-1 and Action 123

Section Three: The Turnaround You 135

The New You - Who Are You Now? 137

"D.E.S.I.R.E" ™- The Formula 145

Foreword

If you are ready for a change in your life and hold yourself responsible for that change, this book *"How to Turn Your Pain to Power"* is for you.

This book is loaded with principles, strategies and keys that when applied, can radically change your situation. If you're at the place where you feel uncomfortable with your present achievements, then this is a tool to help you turn it around and bring you to a new dimension. This book places emphasis on the fact that the day you discover your purpose is the day you'll stop existing and start living.

The author makes this an easy to read book, which is practical and full of real-life experiences.

Thanks for making this resource available for such a time as this. If you say, "enough is enough," then this is a must-read book for you.

Revd. Dr Joel M. Thomas, D.Th
International Overseer
Church of God World Wide Mission International

" Deep within man dwell those slumbering powers; powers that would admonish him, that he never dreamed of possessing; forces that would revolutionize his life if aroused and put into action."

Orison Swett Marden

Introduction

You can take a twenty-dollar bill, jump on it, spit on it, curse it then rub it in the dirt; guess what? The twenty-dollar bill is still valuable, still worthy, still useable and is still a twenty-dollar bill. It has not lost any of its value because of what it has been through. This twenty-dollar bill can still continue to transact business for you as usual, without anyone knowing what it has endured, and the journey it has travelled.

This is not about the money. This is about the painful life events that we have all endured at some time in our lives that left us feeling less than valuable, less than worthwhile and less humane. You may have been spat on, jumped on, cursed, reduced to dirt, but know this; you are still valuable, and you still have worth. Like the twenty-dollar bill, you didn't ask for this treatment, but unlike the twenty-dollar bill, you have to address the scars and the hole left in your soul from the treatment you received. When you address the scars, you will begin a live a powerful life not a powerless existence.

I am here to admonish you that whatever may have happened, your past does not equal your future. You may have made mistakes, but you are not a mistake. There is a way to make the past be the past; there is a way to turn the pain of the past into power for your future. If you want to turn around your life to a place of power where you maximise your potential and live a fulfilled life, this book is for you.

I write this book to encourage you whilst you're in a place of pain. You must know, this pain will not last, but it too shall pass. The emptiness you now feel because of something that has happened in your past is temporary. The good news is you will laugh again, you will love again, and you will start to live again.

Being down does not mean you are out. You are still in the race called life. As long as there is breath in your body you can rise and fight another day. You are wiser, stronger, better and bolder than any current or future crisis that will knock at your door. Yes, you may have cried into the darkness of the night, and yes, there may have been many tears on your pillow and negative whispers that say you are finished, that was a lie.

You have just started your journey to turn your life around. In you is the ability to bounce back, and I will show you how, based on the principles I have researched, used and found to be successful in my own life. You are about to put on eagles' wings and soar to new heights you have not previously imagined. This is because of a crisis, an adversity, a heartbreak, or something that caused you much personal pain.

Pain is an indicator that something is wrong and when you experience pain, be it physical or emotional, it is a call for action. There is no better champion in life than a man or woman who remained positive and triumphant despite the personal pain they carry.

The pain of a crisis will come to everyone at some time in his or her live. It is in the midst of a crisis that giants are born, that champions emerge, that overcomer's triumph. According to Albert Einstein "The purpose of a crisis is to expose a man to himself." When the rubber hits the road, a crisis will separate the men from the boys and the women from the girls. Whatever you have been through, are going through, or will go through in the future, life will ask you a question "who are you?" Are you the weak or the strong; are you the follower or the leader? Do you have the right answer?

Now is your time to make a full commitment to move forward, to transform your life and live it to the fullest of your potential. Now is the time to break through the barriers, which have stopped your progress. Now is the time to recognise the God-given brilliance within you. As you read this book, I will speak of some of my experiences, which stopped me in my tracks for years, existing only but not living. Today, I am no longer stuck; my weakness has become my strength, and my pain has become my power.

I use my experiences of the past to deliver principles that will liberate you right now. Not only to liberate now, but to get you to live your life on purpose with a purpose. Now that's turning pain to power, and that's the gift I want to give you.

I write this book to encourage those who have wings but cannot fly, those who are weeping not knowing that joy will come in the morning. For those who are mourning not knowing they will be dancing tomorrow, for those enduring emotional pain not knowing that their pain is the secret to their power. Where you are right now, is temporary and is subject to change.

This book is remind you that you will make it; you are an overcomer; you will not die but you will live to tell your story of your history. Be assured your experiences are never wasted. The foundation of personal power is to be able to survive and thrive because of the pain you have carried.

My hope for you is that from today on, you will make a commitment to yourself to commence this transformational journey, so the pain from your past can become the power for your future.

Get ready to turn your pain into power!

Section One:
Turning on You. What's going on?

CHAPTER ONE

ABC- Admit, Beware, Compare

The only source of knowledge is experience. - Albert Einstein

It's not what happens to you, but how you react to it that matters. - Epictetus

Admit where you are right now

Many people are stuck in life because of a painful event of the past that impacted them negatively. It could be any type of crisis; something unexpected like a death, abuse, car accident, redundancy, insurmountable debts, disappointment, natural disaster, divorce, terminal illness, or the like. Experiencing such crisis can cause a devastating negative reaction within us, which can last for generations. If left unaddressed, many carry the wounds and scars for decades. Many lived empty unproductive and unfulfilled lives; dying at age thirty but were not buried until age seventy. This is because they were unable to recover from the wounds of the past.

Many have become stuck in life, unable to move forward, trying to let go of the despair, whilst reaching for a future. Others take two steps forward and three backwards, and never make any real progress to rebuild the shattered pieces of their lives.

It will take a methodical approach to be free. Before you can start to fix anything, you have to admit that you have a problem and why it needs fixing. When you take your car to the garage, the mechanic will ask you to describe what is happening to the car, and how is it behaving and reacting? In other words, what are the symptoms? It is necessary for him to understand what is happening to the car before it can be fixed. In my own life, I have taken my car to the garage thinking it was one problem only to be told by the expert it's something else.

Once you admit something is wrong, it's necessary to be honest about the real issues; otherwise, there could be a misdiagnosis of the issue. This means the remedy will not work. To start the process, you must be aware of what is happening in you, admit it and understand it, so you can begin the process of turning it around. You might pretend on the outside that all is well, but your body is so wonderfully and fearfully made that it will produce symptoms to get your attention that something is wrong. You may have buried what you feel, but that doesn't mean it is dead.

Your body is speaking, are you listening?

You must become aware of the symptoms that are occurring in your body, because of the problems in your life. Symptoms are a sign that something is wrong. They should not be ignored, but are there as a guide to tell you to address the root causes.

When you experience an unexpected event of extreme proportion, your physical body and your psyche are involved in the way you respond. Your psyche consists of your mind, soul and spirit. The resulting symptoms, which the pain of the crisis can manifest, may be evident in either your physical body or in your psyche (emotions and behaviours). You must become aware of symptoms that are being produced in your body and your psyche before you can even think about a remedy to turn it around.

How your body speaks physically

Here are some of the physical symptoms you might notice:

- Aches and pains
- Over sleeping or/and not sleeping enough
- Over eating or/and not eating enough
- Unexpected growths in the body
- Lethargy and fatigue
- Low or no energy

How your body speaks emotionally

Here are some of the emotional symptoms you might notice:

- Despair
- Negative thoughts and words
- Depression, bitterness and anger
- Guilt
- Blame
- Forgetfulness
- Isolation from others
- Social withdrawal
- Irritability
- Mood swings
- Suicidal thoughts
- Inability to forgive
- Consistent lateness

The list is not endless, but I can tell you at some time in my life I experienced most of these. You must understand that the human body is far too intelligent to produce these symptoms without a reason. This is the body's way of telling you that you are out of balance. It is an alarm bell, which should get your attention and your response. Don't just aim to treat the effect, you must also understand the cause of what happened in your life when you started to feel aches, pain, and mood swings. You must diagnose the real reason.

Compare what your body is saying to how you want to feel

When you compare how you feel to how you would like to feel, and there is a sizeable gap, then there is a problem. Above and beyond any advice in this book, if you can identify with any of the above symptoms, please seek medical help immediately.

It is difficult to expect people to understand how you feel or what you are going through. Many will tell you "just get over it." If it were that easy, we'd all do it, right? Many will tell you they had to get over "whatever," so you should too.

If you scratch beneath the surface of these advisors, you will find that many are still the walking wounded. They have teeth but no bite, heart but no feelings, sympathy but no compassion. They mean well, but they are still hurting. You cannot receive healing from a wounded advisor, no more than a poor man can teach you how to be rich. Until the poor becomes rich, his voice is silenced on the matter.

Einstein said, "We cannot solve our problems with the same level of thinking we had when we created them." First, you will need to admit you have a problem. Second, you need to have an awareness of the events that got you there. Third, you need to get to a deeper level of understanding in order to remedy the problem. Einstein is right!

Why is your body talking physically and emotionally?

For every cause, there is an effect. In other words, if you feel sad or happy, there is a reason for it. In the workplace, this is referred to as a root cause analysis. If you analyse how you feel right now, you will find it is caused by your thoughts of an event or something that has happened in the past or is happening now, be it good or bad.

Over the past decade, I have had a number of life-changing events that had put my life on hold for years. In hindsight, these events were just a setup for me to discover deeper wells of knowledge for turning painful events into a powerful life.

About eight years ago I had a sudden life-threatening illness. The background was that I went to Jamaica to celebrate my Gran's 90th birthday. A few days after arrival, there was a forecast of a maximum category five hurricane. The predictions for loss of life and damage were horrendous. We did all the preparations; we placed sandbags on the roof, boarded up the windows, removed any potential flying objects, and did all the chores that needed to be done.

There was an eerie and uneasy calm in the atmosphere and all around us as the electricity was cut off and we reverted to oil lamps. We waited patiently for the hurricane to arrive.

Hurricane Dean arrived with all the aggression of a pack of hungry lions ripping apart a carcass. Dean hit the Island with 140 mph winds and tore most of the roof off the house. This left me, my Gran and my family running for shelter and dear life. We huddled together in one room, where water came through making the walls vibrate like jelly. This lasted for about 15 hours, and we survived with no loss of life. I believe this was a miracle.

Within those 15 hours, my brother and I broke the fear barrier. We got to a point where we came out from the safety of the one room and walked through the house with debris on the floor, flying debris in the air and no roof. It was pitch black; all we had was a battery-powered torch. In hindsight, it became obvious that during our walk, we were both in shock. After the hurricane was over the devastation was appalling, the trees were flattened, we could see for miles and the roof, which came off our house, was found some four miles away. Within 36 hours, I was out of the country and back in the UK.

On return to the UK, I was diagnosed with PTSD (Post Traumatic Stress Disorder) and malaria. The doctors informed me I had all the symptoms of someone returning from a war zone. I was in bed for six months, and it took 12 months to return to normal life. During this time of severe illness, I was made redundant from my job.

I had worked faithfully for the organisation and spent many years turning it into a profit leader. After years of commitment, late nights and personal sacrifice, I was to be made redundant whilst I was sick with PTSD and malaria. Like the twenty-dollar bill, I didn't ask for this to happen, and I didn't expect it to happen, but it did.

Just reading the letters about redundancy triggered off a whole range of aches and pain, negative thought patterns and mood swings, as my health deteriorated. I was like an airplane out of control. I felt physically and emotionally stuck as I contended with what I felt. I was already incapacitated and bed ridden and like the twenty-dollar bill, I didn't ask for this to happen. The timing of everything was not perfect, so I had to find a way to deal with it, even from a sick bed.

How the physical and emotional symptoms got worse

I spent time reflecting on how I turned the organisation around, the many long days and nights that I worked nonstop, and the family appointments and dates that I missed because of work. Needless to say, I found myself depressed, in despair and angry. The worst I felt, the more the malaria ravished my body.

For every cause, there was an effect. The more negative my thoughts were, the worse the illness and my misery became. I felt helpless and powerless to act because of my health, or so I thought at the time.

I had a problem and nothing would change until I admitted I had a problem. I had to sound the alarm and said "Houston, I have a problem." I was getting weaker and weaker, and the doctors reported that my blood was being depleted of oxygen. The more frustrated and annoyed I became about my employment, the worst the build-up of toxicity within the blood.

What was driving this? It was not the malaria; it was my thoughts, my negative conversations. I will never forget an imaginary conversation I had rehearsed in my head that I would "have it out" with my boss. This conversation went on in my head and was as real as if he was in my room standing over my bed. Afterwards, I remember getting up to try to make it to the bathroom, and I fell on the floor.

As a result of this imaginary conversation, my blood had become so toxic that my pores opened to release the toxicity through sweat. By the time I was taken off the floor, it looked like a crime scene. There was just a wet outline of sweat on the floor where I fell. Had I not been ill, I probably would not have been so observant about what was going on within me.

I had to admit, I had a problem that I did not want. Nothing will change until you confess your current state; because this becomes your starting point to turn things around.

Compare where you are to where you want to be

I was ill with malaria and PTSD, and about to be made redundant. Fear, doubt and negativity had taken hold as I wrestled with my situation.

I had a photo album of my happier days and I started to wonder if those days would ever return again. My emotions were up and down like a palm tree on a windy day. The more I looked at the photos, the more I compared how I was, to how I would like to be again. The power of vision took over my life. I focused on the possibility of a better and brighter future although I did not know what it entailed.

I started to think of the possibility of life and laughter again. This was only the start, but this was a good place to be. I will take you on my journey in the proceeding chapters, on how I started and completed the journey through life threatening illness, redundancy, family bereavement and much more. It is not about what has happened to you but how you respond to it that matters.

This ABC concept is Biblical

It is a natural and biblical concept to admit you have a problem. Be aware of the symptoms within, and compare where you are now to where you want to be in the future. In the Bible, Jesus encountered a blind man, but before he offered him anything, Jesus asked him "What do you want?" The blind man replied that he would like to receive his sight[i]. In simple terms, the man admitted he was blind, he could not see and what he required was to be able to see as normal. You can't assume you know what people want until you ask and you can't help a person who doesn't want your help. Have you been able to admit that you have a problem? Are you aware of the symptoms being produced in your body by your perception of the problem? Do you know what you want?

You have to be mindful of people who tell you to "just get over it." Such people still have a tendency to experience the emotions related to their pain as if the incident took place yesterday. Time by itself does not always heal. You can only turn misery to mastery and pain to power by the application of time-tested strategies, principles and keys.

It is important to understand that it's not what happens to you, but how you respond to it that really matters. The power to make this switch lies within you. Once you discover how to do this, you can use these methods over and over again in your life to break through the pain of the past. You don't have to be controlled by circumstances, people or situation. By applying the time-tested strategies in this book you will discover the hidden treasure within you, where you can turn your pain to power.

The power is always on the inside of you

According to Alice Walker, "The most common way people give up their power is by thinking they don't have power." I assure you, you have more power in you than you can ever dream, think or imagine. You will survive to laugh, live and love again. You have the power to change, to be better, and to live a fulfilled live.

When I look back on my life, I would not change a thing. I now realise that the many crises I faced made me into a woman of passion, purpose and power. According to Bruce Lee, "Knowledge gives you power, but character earns you respect."

You will discover that when you make the effort to be better, you will develop your own self-respect and then the respect of others. This is because it takes adversity, obstacles, and crises to mould and build character. If I had not endured adversity and conquered it, I would not be writing this book to help you. Now that's taking pain and turning it into power!

As from today, tell yourself " there will be no more regrets." You will no longer be stuck in a rut, but you are coming out to take charge of your life. Have an attitude of gratitude, because you are on a journey, which will change your life for good.

You are about to undergo a metamorphosis like the caterpillar into the butterfly. You may look like a moth at present, but you are about to enter a cocoon and days from now emerge into a new person, full of life, full of purpose, full of power, and full of beauty.

A powerful lesson from the Chinese

In the Chinese language, the same letter that is used to depict danger is also used to depict opportunity. In other words, according to the Chinese culture, crisis presents a threat or a danger, but likewise, it presents an opportunity for expansion and growth.

Can you see it's about perception?

How do you perceive the challenge before you? Do you see it as a danger or opportunity for growth?

Life may have thrown you a lemon; you can complain about the bitterness, or you can make some lemonade. The choice is yours.

What I have learnt about the pain of a crisis is that it is how you respond to it, which determines whether the crisis controls you or whether you remain in control during the crisis.

Did you see the Paralympics in 2012? Did you listen to the stories of what people had to overcome to be world champions? Did you hear the stories of amputations, birth defects, rejections at birth? Yet, these great men and women did not allow the pain of the situation, nor the rejection of others to stop them becoming all that they wanted to be.

They used their disadvantage to their advantage; they turned their pain into their power. You can too!

You may have heard of Leonardo Da Vinci, that well-known painter of the mystery lady Mona Lisa with her endearing smile. The truth about Da Vinci was that he was the product of a broken and dysfunctional home. He was labelled by the world as an illegitimate child who never knew his mother. Needless to say, his childhood was miserable, but he had a vivid imagination on which he thrived and survived.

As Da Vinci matured, he began to understand the God-given dreams inside him. He progressed to become a leading illustrator, sculptor, botanist, engineer, anatomist and astronomer of the fifteen and sixteenth centuries. Today his works are considered to be masterpieces and they consistently set records at art auctions.

What has stopped you? What have you allowed to limit your potential?

When I came to the UK my English was so poor the headmaster of the college refused me entry due to poor language skills. I persevered, cried tears at his feet and, out of his compassion, he granted me entry

Three years later I left with the highest awards in my class.

How desperate are you for a breakthrough? How desperate are you for a change? You must need a breakthrough like the desert needs the rain, and your lungs need air. This book is your opportunity for new doors to open and for you to pioneer new paths.

There are keys which athletes and countless others used to overcome the vicissitudes of life. Benjamin Disraeli says, "Circumstances are beyond human control, but our conduct towards them is our own personal power." Wow! In other words, it is how you respond to the uncontrollable that reveals the depth of your personal power.

After you have been through this book, you will no longer stand on the shore being afraid of two inches of water, but you will launch out into the deep.

Someone said that winning starts with beginning. You have taken the first step; continue on this journey and don't give up until you win. Let's carry on.

Points to ponder and act upon before you leave this section

1. *What problem do you currently have?*

   ----

2. *What physical symptoms do you have in your body as a result of that problem?*

   ----

3. *What emotional symptoms do you have in your body as a result of that problem?*

   ----

4. *Can you link the start of the symptoms with the problem and in what way?*

   ----

5. *What are your perceptions about what happened to you?*

   ----

6. How can you give a more empowering meaning to what has happened? Where do you want to be?

   ----

7. List 10 empowering meanings/perceptions that you can give to the crisis that happened?

CHAPTER TWO

To Thine own Self Be True

To thine own self be true. - William Shakespeare

Then you shall know the truth and the truth shall set you free. - John 8:32

Be true to you

You cannot camouflage what you are really feeling; you have to uncover and confront the truth, otherwise you will end up putting a plaster on the gunshot wound of your life. You cannot change what you will not confront. You might lie to others, but to thine own self you must be true.

You have crossed the first hurdle and have acknowledged the physical and emotional symptoms within you, and that for every cause there is an effect. You have realised that you have a problem. The next step is to address the main vices of denial, anger, and acceptance, to shift from misery to mastery, and become all you want to be. I have focused on anger in this book because it was the dominant controlling factor in my life. However, I am aware that for others it might be fear, depression, guilt, or worry which are all topics in their own right. The same process can be used irrespective of the dominant factor in your life.

When you look inwards at what has happened, you will need to consider and address the lies you have believed and the self-limiting beliefs you have formed because of your environment or experiences. To get to where you want to go, you must start the journey from where you are. You have to confront what is going on inside of you, in order to have dominion over what is going on outside of you. It starts inside out; the journey starts from within.

You have to transition from excuses and blame to take 100% responsibility for yourself. Are you refusing to take 100% responsibility for yourself and your actions? Was it the mosquito's fault? Was it my boss' fault? Is it easier to focus blame on someone else rather than accept responsibility for yourself and what you can change.

Will you continue to pass the buck or will you deal with it?

There is story in John 5 about a man who was sick for thirty eight years. Once per year an angel would stir up the water in the pool and the first person to enter would be healed. One day, Jesus visited the pool and asked the sick man "Will you be made whole?" The man started to explain that he had no one to help him and every time he tried to enter the pool someone would step ahead of him. This man had every reason to be angry and he probably was, but in reality he had thirty eight years of excuses as to why he was not healed.

What is your excuse? Will you allow another year to past by whilst you blame others and the system for your condition? How many years of excuses do you have? The question that was asked by Jesus required a "yes "or "no" answer but the man gave excuse after excuse in reply to the question.

Surely, he could have asked someone else to help him into the pool or he could have sat at the edge of the pool and rolled in, but instead he had his excuses. However, Jesus had compassion on him and healed him from his sickness.

I know the questions asked are harsh and I would not in any way belittle your pain; however, until you challenge yourself with the truth, you will not move on and become whole in the process. Like the twenty dollar bill, you are still full of value and full of worth irrespective of what has happened to you or what you have been through.

If you have considered these questions, then you have started to face the truth about what you believe, and why you feel the way you do. If that is the case, as you read on, you will start to:

- Figure out what you want out of life.
- Break down the barriers of denial.
- Understand what is making you angry, and learn how to release yourself from these negative emotions.
- Confront and release yourself from the limiting beliefs that have made you stuck.

You must challenge what you think with real hard facts, and find an explanation for the turmoil within. Excuses are not acceptable to move you from a place of pain to power. Excuses have a habit of shifting the focus off you and putting it on someone else. To be free to live the life you have always wanted, the spotlight must remain solely on you.

I could not control my boss, I could not control the hurricane, I could not control the mosquito n or the malaria. I could not control the death of my Gran, all that I could control was my response. My response is inclusive of my thoughts, beliefs, emotions and behaviors.

Lies deflate, truth liberates

When I was informed that I would be made redundant, at first I could not believe it. I felt like I had been slapped in the face by a fishing net. My body had no means to express the toxic emotions I carried whilst already sick, and although I kept a lid on it, my body started to break down. I wasted much-needed energy and time being in denial, with anger, and sadness which changed absolutely nothing about my situation.

The question which had the most negative impact was "what if I never work again?" This thought was my constant companion for weeks, morning, noon and night. I was never alone without it.

The medical report stated that I would be incapacitated for 6-12 months and I was in bed wallowing in self-pity.

I had faith that I would be healed, but I had no faith that I would find gainful employment. Fear had made an entrance when I was at my weakest, and I had laid out a table, invited fear in and entertained it. Every week, the doctor's report got worse; perhaps it was a mirror image of what was happening in my mind.

One night, just before dawn, I started one of the most amazing and all inspiring self-talks. In brief, I found myself saying, "Rose, you are a qualified accountant and auditor. You speak good English. You articulate well and someone out there must need your skills-set."

In the midst of my despair, in the complete feeling of hopelessness, still needing help to get off the bed, I started saying, "use what you got Rose- you have something - use it." This was my turn around moment.

I may have been ill in my body, but I still had a sound mind. All along, I was being led by my situation of sickness and redundancy, not my revelation of who I was as a person. This is important. Everybody has a gift, if you can speak, dance, act, write, entertain, then all you have to do is plan to use what you have. You have something - you have to dig deep and be honest with yourself, but you have something.

My liberation started when I acknowledged that redundancy was a reality I had to face. Redundancy may have stopped my employment, but redundancy could not stop me. In other words, nothing changed in my world until I took 100% responsibility for my feelings, my destiny and myself.

This is your personal power, and if you have lost it, you must find it and take it back. Your destiny cannot be left at the beck and call of others, it must be left in your hands.

From that moment, the weight started to lift and I started to feel better and better with the passing of each day. Why? I didn't deny the fact of redundancy; I just defied its impact. One small but powerful thought caused me to launch my consulting business and from then, I never looked back.

What I thought was the end, was just a bend in my life, as I used truth to challenge my own negative thinking and turned misery to mastery and pain to power. You shall know the truth, and the truth shall set you free[ii]. Once you know the truth, you will discover that road to success is a journey and not a one-off event.

You cannot control circumstances and people; you can only control yourself. Re-write your script and acknowledge the truth about you.

Somebody said, "It is easier to move from failure to success than to move from excuses to success." This means, others have become your excuse for lack of progress and success. It is sad for anyone to give their personal power away to excuses or to someone else. Find an empowering thought that is true about yourself and use it as a weapon against the negative thoughts. Repeat it to yourself over and over until the seed of change takes hold in the fertility of your mind.

The same effort it takes to come up with excuses, is the effort it takes to think positively to make changes in your life. You have to break the habit of excuses and put yourself at the centre of your life. If you are blaming someone for how you feel right now, you are in denial. You have given away your personal power to the situation or person. They have become your proactive driver, and you are the inactive passenger living by fate and not faith. You cannot drive your car from the back seat. Something or someone must change; there must be a shift, a repositioning, a turning around, so you drive yourself to your destiny.

You must reposition yourself to become the Lewis Hamilton of your vehicle to success. Whilst others are in the driving seat, they can drive you to distraction, destruction, desperation and depression. When you are in control of the vehicle to your destiny, you can drive it to prosperity, peace, purpose and power.

No one can have your interest at heart like you can. You must be the front-seat driver of your life. In other words, you must become the Michael Angelo of your life and the Choir Director of your future. You must be in command, you have the power within and you must use it and not delegate it.

Don't deny but defy.

When you receive bad news, or a series of it, you can become numb to the reality, just as I did with being made redundant. Some have a delayed reaction to the news they receive, whilst others refuse to accept reality. This refusal to accept reality is called denial.

Denial that is not dealt with, will pursue you and deal with you swiftly and severely until you face reality. Many people at times of their lives go through seasons of denial, unable to face the truth for what it is.

Denial in simple terms is refusing to face or acknowledge unpleasant facts. This can become so debilitating, that you neither move backwards or forwards, you are just existing but not really living.

As human beings, we use denial as a way to lessen the emotional intensity of what we actually feel. We separate ourselves from our emotions to lessen the blow. A marriage could be going through great turmoil, whilst one party is pretending everything is great; the other is planning a divorce. Not to face the state of the marriage, is to suppress the reality privately to help cope with what you feel.

Your emotions can only be suppressed for so long before they rise to the surface. Denial is not just about what has happened to you, it is also about what is happening inside you. Just because you have buried the painful emotion doesn't mean it is dead. What it means is that they have been buried "alive." Anything that is buried alive has a nasty habit of showing up when you least expect it. Buried emotions do not rise to the surface calmly and gently.

Your conscious, unconscious and subconscious self knows when you are in denial! Your body knows the truth, and will act out until your fantasy lines up with the reality of what has happened.

Denial of facts is a dreadful thing, which leaves you powerless. I recall a friend who was planning her elaborate and expensive wedding, whilst knowing that the relationship was already in dire straits. The marriage was destined to fail. She was more in love with the idea of getting married and was in denial of the facts.

She went ahead with the wedding and within weeks, the marriage had ended. The writing was on the wall, but she had stopped reading.

I have known friends who were being laid-off work, but continued with lavish spending sprees as if nothing had happened. Or the person, who suffered a sudden death in the family, but puts on a brave face and after the funeral, when all the visitors have gone, became depressed. Such people need to be helped not criticized.

So what's your story? If you are reading this book, I know you can identify with it. If it's not a story from your childhood, it is one from you "current hood." The biggest favour you can do for yourself, is to decide that enough is enough, and that your time has come to make a definite change.

I was one such person who was in denial for weeks when my Gran died. I had to travel abroad to the Caribbean for the funeral, but I remember my husband handling all the flight arrangements. At my request, he booked for us to arrive the night before the funeral.

What happened was that I was in denial, I didn't want to face reality. Denial is a self-destruct button. It is a cover up for the reality we must face. It is the equivalent of the three brass monkeys, "hear no," "see no," and "speak no."

I had only spoken to my Gran a few days before she died, and was told that she was doing well. I never expected her passing so soon afterwards; I thought she would live. I am not sure what causes us to think a person will just live and live and live. I saw her bounce back from so many crises, I never prepared myself for her passing.

I have come to realise that whether a death is expected or unexpected, it does not lessen the emotional pain, which drives many into denial. It was when I returned to the UK that reality caught up with me. I was under my duvet for weeks, working it all out and coming to terms with her passing. I had to work on my thoughts and beliefs, to drive my emotions to help with the denial and subsequent bereavement process. I discuss these in detail in the upcoming chapters.

So what are you in denial about? What facts have you refused to face? What lies have you accepted as truth? How do you plan to address the lies you have lived by, with the truth you now know?

Manage your anger

Many times when something has gone drastically wrong, you can find yourself harbouring feelings of anger, particularly if the situation is outside of your control. Anger is a feeling that most people experience, even a child. It is common to the human race, and is usually spurned on by being in unpleasant circumstances. Anger is an automatic response to unfair treatment and is a way for a person to indicate that he or she will no longer tolerate certain types of behaviour. Many people have stored up anger because of a past event.

The manifestations of anger can be seen in agitations, facial expressions, aggression, body language, and so on. The behaviours associated with anger are designed to warn aggressors to stop their threatening actions.

Since my childhood, I had an anger problem, and I realised it could be harmful to me and the people around me. I wasn't born angry; I was crying when I came out of the womb, but I hope I wasn't crying angrily. This anger was an indication that I had pent-up emotions that had not been resolved and which I had buried.

Between the ages of three and sixteen, I had changed countries twice, changed schools five times, changed homes twice, and changed guardians and friends. It was not a surprise to find that with all those changes, I was carrying the battle scars of anger.

This anger was lying dormant, awaiting resurrection or public viewing. I could see the colour red in a flash, quicker than the speed of light, and I knew I was a walking time bomb. I read the traditional self-help books and attended anger management sessions. As a result, my anger would die for a couple of days, but then came back in full force.

I went to a life mastery seminar, with thousands of people from all walks and nationalities of life. I recall the Team Leader for my group asking if anyone had a negative emotion they wanted to change in their lives.

My hand was the first to go up, and as she pointed me out I said, "I would want to keep cool in difficult situations." The first thing I did was to admit I had a problem – I was no longer in denial about it. Secondly, I knew what I wanted, but I was being guarded with the diagnosis of the problem. The team leader was very candid and asked, "Rose, do you have an anger problem?" I said, "yes" angrily. The truth was out; it was mandatory for me to change. Anger is a natural feeling, it wasn't anger that I had a concern with. It was what I would and could do when I got very angry that was scary. We can be angry but it should not turn into tempestuous actions[iii].

Many times you can think about the things you could have done, or should have done, but did not do. Until it becomes "a must" in your life, you remain powerless to change it. If you accept it, you will not change it. This is about getting leverage on yourself and making it compulsory for you to change. In other words, the rewards of change, such as health, happiness, joy, peace and fulfillment must outweigh the risk of not changing, i.e. remaining stuck, miserable, sad and depressed. It is the risk versus the reward, or good versus bad challenge of a lifetime which you must face.

One technique used was for the team to keep asking, "What will happen if you don't change from being angry, Rose?" I wasn't given time to think, if I paused the team just kept asking and repeating the question. I just had to come up with answers and keep the flow going. I had answers like "I might hurt someone one day, or someone might hurt me instead, or it will not be good for me." None of these replies had any impact, until out of my mouth came these words, "If I don't change, I will die angry."

That stopped me in my tracks; I broke into pieces; it was like being in a busy super market, and the trolleys stopped, the cash registers stopped, the people stopped, the voices stopped, and all I could observe was the stillness of the silence. My time had come, it was a defining moment, something within me cried out for change from this raging anger I carried.

I had this picture, that when it was my time to go to heaven, people would look and wonder "what happened to her face?" You know that angry face emoticon that was the picture I saw in my mind. I had leverage on myself. This was my wake-up call to change. All along, that power to change was within me, undiscovered and unused. I just didn't know it. I looked for help outside but all along the solution was inside of me. It took a person of understanding to draw it out[iv]. I was free from anger.

Your liberation will be tested

I remember being very charitable to someone I thought needed my help, and I did everything possible to be of assistance. I was terribly let down and disappointed as close friends turned against me. It was a very painful time. This was how I knew I had been liberated from anger. I did not have a slinging match, did not attempt to hit anyone, nor raise my voice or shout at anyone, or tried to explain anything to anyone.

I had conquered the old debilitating horrors of anger without sleepless nights of having to rehearse my apologies, or having to think of excuses to explain away my bad behaviour. Temptations and tests will come; that's only natural and you may have a relapse, but don't forget your journey, don't throw in the towel.

You get up, dust yourself off and consistently persist towards being a better you tomorrow. I have never met a perfect person - have you?

I had to be true to me and acknowledge that if I hadn't helped this person, I would not have suffered as I did. This is where you take responsibility and stop the blame game. I didn't deny the fact, but defied the odds.

Learning from Joseph and his brothers

These instances are not beyond the bounds of possibility. You may know the story of Joseph with his cloak of many colours. Joseph's brothers sold him into slavery because Joseph had a dream of which his brothers were envious. His brothers were also jealous because Joseph was his father's favourite child. The jealous brothers conspired against Joseph and sold him into slavery. They took his coat of many colours, dipped it in animal blood, showed it to their Dad and informed him that Joseph had died at the hands of some ravenous beasts.

Can you imagine how Joseph's Dad must have felt? Can you imagine how Joseph must have felt as he fell from hero to zero and from popular to unpopular. Joseph was hurt by what had happened, but despite his pain, he continued to make progress towards his destiny.

He went from being lowered into a pit, to working in a palace, to being falsely accused and going to prison.

None of this was his fault, and he was an innocent man behind bars. Joseph transitioned through all this, and went from prison, to become an extremely generous and prosperous Prime Minister. You could say he was the equivalent of Nelson Mandela of our day.

Joseph did not sit in prison counting the days, he made every day count towards his purpose. One day Joseph met his brothers and his father again. He revealed that he was alive and not dead. He did not seek revenge, was not angry, did not harbour past hurts, but totally forgave his brothers. He fulfilled his destiny and turned his pain into power.

As long as you continue to blame others, as long as you continue to be angry with others, as long as you cannot forgive, as long as you continue to feel bitter - you are stuck. Joseph dealt with what he felt, and did not allow circumstances beyond his control to stop the fulfillment of his purpose in life.

When you examine Joseph's life, he took all that anger and pain and turned it into power by becoming who he dreamt he would be. You will encounter disappointment on life's journey, which will make you feel angry. Will you use the anger to drive you forward to greater heights, or will you allow the anger to stop you?

Successful people leave clues for us to follow. There are methods for success and there are methods for failure. If you consistently try and fail, you must recognise that failure is a clue that you are not doing the right thing, so you need to do something different. You cannot do the same thing over and over, day in and day out, and expect different results.

You must perform a shift, no matter how small, to get a different result. So what results do you want? What are you willing to do to get the results you desire? What action will you take today to start your journey to success?

Don't beat up yourself about anything. If you made a mistake, deal with it, and start to shift your life from where you are to where you want to be.

Accept to progress

By acceptance, I mean that you perceive reality accurately and consciously acknowledge what you perceive. So, if a death has occurred, you accept it. You become aware of what you are feeling as a result and start to take steps to address what you feel.

George Orwell said, " Happiness can exist only in acceptance." In other words, if you are experiencing difficulties in a particular area of your life, there's a strong chance that the root of the problem is a failure to accept the reality as it is.

The most basic mistake we make is our failure to perceive accurately and accept our present situation. Once you accept it, you can begin to make plans to change your response to it. Until a person accepts they are overweight and knows by how much they are overweight, they will not begin to take the necessary steps to address their weight issue. They will go through denial, angry and depression about their weight, and convince themselves that they are okay. In other words, what you tolerate you will never change.

You have the inner ability to activate the power of acceptance about the current crisis that lives in you. At some point, you must reach a sense of acceptance of the death, the disappointment, the deception, the redundancy, or whatever your problem might be. The sooner this is done, the better.

Acceptance doesn't mean you forget or stop caring. If you try to ignore your feelings, moving through this cycle will be almost impossible. You will remain 'stuck' in anger or depression. Dealing with your emerging emotions will help you come to a point of acceptance.

By doing this, you become empowered and see life and the world around you for what it truly is. This is what acceptance is all about. Your inner turmoil will start to wane once you accept reality. Acceptance is a virtue that doesn't require any form of doing in the "physical sense" of the word; it's a chosen way of being. So I have some questions to ask you:

- Why are you stuck?
- Why are you not living your dream?
- Why are you letting past events steal your future?

- Why are you settling for less when you were made for more?
- Are you being true to you?

Do you have an answer? Socrates said, "the life which is unexamined is not worth living." So examine your life and keep your personal response to the questions above.

Acceptance in action

Helen Keller, at age 19 months, became deaf and blind through no fault of her own. A faithful teacher opened the door to her learning and communication skills, and Helen became the first deaf person to earn a Bachelor of Art's degree. Helen Keller later became a political activist, a legendary lecturer, and prolific writer who taught her generation and generations to come, how to overcome life's obstacles. Like Joseph she accepted what had happened and continued to fulfill her destiny. So what is your story?

You have admitted you have a problem, you have become aware of the systems created and you have compared where you are to where you want to be. However, until you accept 100% responsibility for your future and stop blaming others, you will remain disempowered to make the shift from misery to mastery and pain to power. That's why this chapter was so necessary.

I am sure you may have had some uncomfortable feelings as we took this journey to unravel the truth so that you can be true to yourself. This step is paramount so that you can continue the journey from the right perspective. Someone said, "If you do what you have always done, you will be what you have always been, but to do what you have never done, is to be what you have never been." It's time for change.

Let's continue the journey, as we discover and consider the purpose on the inside of you.

Points to ponder and act upon before you leave this section.

1. *What truth have you refused to face? What truth have you denied?*

   ----

2. *List all the people who are hurting because of your denial*

   ----

3. *How will you challenge your denial of the truth?*

   ----

4. *List 10 reasons why you must change your wrong beliefs or denial of truth?*

   ----

5. What are you currently angry about?

   ----

6. List 10 reasons why it's a **must** for you to stop being angry.

Section Two:

Turning you around

What do you want?

CHAPTER THREE

Born To Do What?

There are two great days in a person's life - the day we were born and the day we discover why. - William Barclay

I know that you can do all things and that no purpose of yours can be restrained. - Job 42:2

There is purpose in everything

Everyone was born on purpose, for a purpose. Everything you see, touch, feel, taste or smell has a purpose. If you smell smoke, you know something is burning so you either get out or put it out - the smoke serves a purpose.

Just look around you, everything is pregnant with purpose and endless possibilities. The plants have a purpose, the door has a purpose, the bus has a purpose, the sun, the moon, the stars all have a purpose.

If things have a purpose, why should you as a human being not have a purpose in life?

You are not here by accident; you are here on purpose for a purpose. Everything that is made is designed to solve a problem. Do you know what problem you were made to solve?

The greatest discovery you will ever make during your lifetime is to discover why you were born. You are not an accident and you are not here by mistake. You are alive at this time to serve this generation with your purpose. There is a unique, special and amazing gift on the inside of you that no one can fulfil like you can. When you use that gift or talent, your personality and everything about you, comes into play and no one can do it like you do. That "it," is your purpose in life.

Your life must have a purpose

If you fail to plan you plan to fail, but before you plan you must know what you are aiming at, i.e. your life's purpose. Without a purpose, life has no passion, no meaning, no juice, and no energy.

This is one of the reasons why many become stuck in life, because their focus is on the past hurts, past failures and past successes. But, where purpose is known, you will find drive and energy for life. This is because the future looks bright whilst the past fades into insignificance. Purpose gives you a reason to rise in the morning, full of hope and enthusiasm.

The Greek work for enthusiasm is en Theos, which means God-like. This means when you have a purpose for which you have enthusiasm, you are being like God. God did everything with a purpose in mind, think about that for a minute. He sent His son Jesus here for a purpose and with a purpose as stated in 1 John 3:8. So the way you live, move and have your being, should be with your purpose in mind.

Purpose is built into your DNA and wrapped around your personality and character traits. Scientists have found that the happiest people in life, are those who are doing what they love. Success leaves clues, so find out what you love and plan to do that. You don't have to go big overnight, just start small and build it one step at a time. The absence of purpose in a person's life can cause stress and even a breakdown.

Research has shown that 80% of people hate their job. By implication, only 20% of the workforce love what they are doing. Is it not surprising to find high levels of stress, depression and hopelessness that so many encounter every day? This is one of the reasons why more and more employers have workforce support, to assist people with getting the right perspective on life. Employers know that happy employees mean better focus, better productivity and better business.

The secret in life is to do what you love and better still, find a way to get paid for it. This way, you plan your life around your purpose and not a pay cheque.

Living a purposeful life

The happiest people on the face of the earth are the ones who are fulfilling their purpose in life. Like everything around us, purpose is being fulfilled effortlessly and naturally. The trees don't try to grow, the plants don't try to flower, nor does the sun try to shine.

What is it that you do without even thinking about it, which requires little of no effort on your part? What is it that you do and achieve so effortlessly, that leaves others gasping at your brilliance? That might be "the thing" you were born to do.

You must know, beyond all shadow of a doubt that you were born on purpose for a purpose. That child whom you are raising now, who knows if you are raising the next Prime Minister or President? This could be the reason you were born.

Who knows if you are teaching the next generation of world changers?

Have you taken the time to look into yourself to identify your purpose in life? What do you love? This could be the answer to why you were born.

Many times when we encounter hardships, challenges and disappointments, we stop living and start existing. We seem to forget that we had started on the journey called purpose and somehow became side-tracked. Taking time out to recover and heal is not unusual and is highly recommended, but to stop the pursuit of your purpose for years because of a crisis is where many become stuck in a rut, and live a life of misery. They know what they should do, but for some reason they don't do what they know. Like a car journey you should never forget you were heading somewhere before an accident occurred.

Finding purpose in pain

Many of the people I have worked with have told me painful stories about their past. After listening, I have always been able to see a more empowering message about their past hurts, particularly how they can use it to help others. The truth is, in every bad situation there is good, if you look for the good, you will find it.

This is how you turn your pain into power. You give a more empowering meaning to the pain you have endured, and you consider how you can turn that pain around and use it to help others.

I can now talk to people who are being or have been made redundant about my personal turn around from redundancy. Do you think people would listen to what I have to say and be inspired? Or do you think they would prefer to listen to someone who has never been made redundant?

I can speak to the bereaved and the downtrodden, and share nuggets of hope and encouragement because of my life experiences.

This is how your take the sting out of pain, and turn it into power by using it to serve others. In other words, I have taken all the negatives of my life and turned them to positives and thus discovered a new passion and purpose in life. Sometimes your purpose in life will come dressed up in pain. It is the pain of my past that resulted in this book and the launch of my public speaking, coaching and mentoring programs.

It was pain that gave me a voice to speak and help others to see that they too can turn pain into power. If I can do it, there is hope for you too because success leaves clues.

Be assured, you can start to turn your situation around today. You are never too old or too young to start. You are alive, and that's a good place to start. Where you are right now, might not be where you want to be, but don't worry, it's all part of the process. When I look back at my life, I realise that all the unpleasantness that I had to endure at the hands of others was part of the process. The heartache, the loneliness, the brokenness, being ignored, overlooked and talked about was part of the process. It gave me a depth of understanding of the pain that others felt, which I did not have before. But most importantly it built my character. It also taught me some lessons I never did find in any book but I have understanding of it because of what I endured.

You can only help others when you are no longer angry and saddened about the past, but have gone through the process of being healed.

As a lay preacher, I have always informed my congregation that bad experiences are never wasted experiences. I could take you through the lives of Jesus, Apostle Paul, King David, Daniel, Peter and Joseph to name a few biblical heroes in order to illustrate this point but let us examine some examples from our own time first.

Nelson Mandela spent 27 years in prison but became Prime Minister of South Africa and an agent of change and forgiveness in a nation torn apart by apartheid. Michael Jordan didn't make it into his schools' baseball team but became the number-one basketball player in the world. President Obama was raised without a Dad but became the first African American president of the USA when it was still thought to be an impossibility. It's all about perception. If you look for the good in any bad situation, you will find it. Wherever you focus the mind, you will find a way to turn your situation around.

Winners never quit

As a child, I was bold about what I wanted to be. From age twelve forward, I was good at mathematics and decided I wanted to be an accountant. I remember telling my brother about this after reading one of his books on Commerce. My Gran's home was full of my uncles' and aunts' old schools books, but none caught my attention like books with figures and calculations.

It took some 28 years before my dream became a reality. During these 28 years, I changed countries, moved house, got married, changed jobs, overcame bereavement, overcame rejection, had a ruptured eardrum to name a few, nevertheless, none of these could kill the dream on the inside.

At my first job, my employers refused my application for study assistance stating I needed to be employed for at least two years. I could have waited, but decided to pay for my accounting technicians' qualification myself, which I did over three years

Afterward, I could not afford to pay for the professional accounting qualification course, so I did an auditor's qualification by home study instead. This still complemented my ultimate goal, and gave me time to work and save the funds I needed.

I worked and saved, worked and saved. My third employer would not provide the sponsorship I needed, so I paid for my professional accounting qualifications myself. It was frustrating to hear "no" on every occasion. But when you have a purpose, you will find a way.

Because I paid for the course myself, I could not afford to fail. I had no money for re-sits. I had to pass the first time as my dream and my money were on the line. It took 28 years from the time of decision for my dream to become a reality, but I never gave up.

Your purpose will never leave you. On this journey, I have had personal battles to overcome from broken heartedness, illnesses and challenges with friends. I could have walked away, I could have settled for what was easy. I could have come up with all the excuses why I didn't make it. I was just persistent in pursuit of my dream.

My purpose was too powerful for me to walk away. Even today, I use my accounting qualifications to coach, mentor and run public speaking events on wealth creation principles in particular, how to transition from debt to savings and then to financial independence.

Don't ever give up

Having a crisis on route to your purpose is no reason to abandon your journey. In other words, your journey may not be straightforward, but don't give up and don't give in; always move forward towards your purpose. Find a way to use the accident or the channel to fuel your passion, to get back on track with your purpose. You must become a person of purpose. Your success, your joy, your passion, is tied to you being relentless about your purpose.

I agree that life happens, and stuff happens, but that doesn't have to stop you from achieving your purpose. I have never met a successful person who did not encounter challenges in life. It is the challenges that turn a test into a testimony and a mess into a message.

It is the overcoming that makes the success sweeter and life more rewarding. It's the staying down when you are knocked down that leads to stress and depression, and the rising up that leads to the joys of life.

A lesson from the fleas we should all avoid

You must have heard the story about the Flea Trainer. The trainer in the flea circus noticed some unusual but predictable habits of the fleas. The fleas were trained by putting them in a cardboard box with a lid on top. The fleas would jump up and down and hit the top of the lid of the box repeatedly.

As time went by, the Flea Trainer noticed something very unusual. The fleas would continue to jump, but they were not jumping high enough to hit the lid of the box.

The Flea Trainer then opened the box. When the lid was removed, the fleas continued to jump, but they would not jump out of the box. The fleas had memory recall of the pain they encountered when they tried to jump higher. The purpose of jumping was to escape to freedom but due to the memory of past events, they remained in captivity even when the door was wide open for them to be free. The fleas were just existing, not really living. They were just going through the motions of life, because they had forgotten their purpose for jumping.

What is stopping you from fulfilling your purpose? What past memory is holding you captive? What is that great purpose that you have put on hold because of a past hurt? Your future is too bright to be living in the past. It's time to escape the rut and make a run towards your purpose. That gift inside you is crying out for an expression. When you express it, you will be free from the pain that holds you, and the misery that torments you.

You cannot afford to forget why you are here on earth at this time. Now is the time to come out of the box, put aside the excuses and take responsibility for your destiny.

Could you be abusing your purpose?

Where purpose is unknown, abuse is inevitable. I found myself in this position during seasons on my journey. I will never forget being at the crossroads in my life. Rejection, criticism, disappointment and the broken heartedness of my experiences left me stuck. Jumping but not reaching, existing but not living.

I became a heavy drinker and smoker in my attempt to medicate the pains and disappointment of life. I have learnt that you cannot medicate your emotions. When you finish the medication, the emotions will return and this is how many unknowingly became addicts, because they have not addressed the pain within.

I was a high achiever but felt unfulfilled, something was missing that no job, friend or drug could fill. One Sunday morning, I decided to break with the routine of life and do something different because I wanted a different result. I decided that I would go to church.

The day was wet, windy and bleak. Even the trees looked miserable, and I thought at first I would not go, I would leave it for another day. I had dressed in black to match the day and my mood, still I pushed myself to go.

I drove 17 miles to this church and as I drove by the doors I heard the most angelic singing I have ever heard. I put out my cigarette, sprayed perfume everywhere, and filled my mouth with mints. I abandoned my car, placed a sticky note which read "doctor on call" as I ran through the doors of the church, smelling like a perfumery, whilst trying to act all normal. Can you picture it?

I know you have never done anything so crazy. I was greeted with a warm welcome, and accompanied to a seat not far from the front. It was surreal. Twenty years prior to this I had only been to church for christenings, weddings and funerals, but this was unlike anything I had ever experienced. The Choir was singing its last song, but it was enough to encourage me to stay for the rest of the service.

The Pastor preached a message I think entitled "come up higher." In that message, he talked about knowing your purpose in life, living your purpose and defying the odds to maximise your potential in life. I sat there and listened as every word registered in me like the Ten Commandments on tablets of stone.

By the time Pastor Joel M. Thomas of the Globe, Reading UK had finished, something had happened to me and in me. Something started to unlock within me. I felt peace where I had torment and joy where I had sorrow. I could not explain it. I went to the church a smoker, but from the end of the service until today I remained a non- smoker.

In his message, he stated that where purpose is not known abuse is inevitable. What happened to me? I discovered my purpose in life. My purpose was to be an inspirational teacher, coach, mentor and educator in the turnaround space. To do this requires a voice. I was destroying my voice with nicotine.

Where purpose is unknown, abuse is inevitable. That was over a decade ago, and that expression left such an impression on my life that a decade later I am still at that church, a new, transformed and passionate Christian, living my purpose on purpose.

Purpose will give you an unquenchable zest for life. Since then, I have increased my philanthropic work helping underprivileged children in Africa and India, and mentoring individuals who want to turn their lives around. Also, I obtained a BA (Hons) Pastoral Ministry and preach most Sundays.

You must discover the reason for your existence, put a plan together to fulfill it and deploy your plan like a missile with precision and accuracy. The word "discover" means to:

- Search out
- Give meaning to
- Establish the characteristics of.
- Work out your boundaries and limits.

This means that when you discover your purpose, it:

- Gives your life meaning.
- Helps you develop you character to match your purpose.
- Helps you to determine what you will and will not do to fulfill your purpose?

When you think about a Priest, you will have formed an opinion about his life, his characteristics and the boundaries of his life. It's the same when you think about a racing car driver or a politician because they know their purpose. Similarly, when you discover your purpose, it will start to shape your character and set the boundaries for your life.

Your purpose on earth is designed to meet a need, which is the same as solving a problem. Where purpose is unknown, abuse is inevitable so you must know your purpose in life. I have listed some biblical characters and things about them to see if any of their life stories resonate with you:

- Moses' purpose was to be the deliverer to the Children of Israel, which consisted of over three million people. Moses got involved in fight, attempting to deliver one man and in so doing committed murder. Moses went in hiding until God helped him refined his character. It was only then that Moses fulfilled his purpose.
- The Woman at the Well[v] had a purpose, which was to bring an entire city of men to Christ. Instead, she became so fascinated by men that she married and divorced five of them and was co-habiting with number six. When she realised her purpose, she fulfilled her purpose and brought the men of the city to have an encounter with Christ.
- The Woman by the name of Rahab[vi] became a prostitute. Her purpose was to bring a Godly seed within the linage of Jesus Christ. Her search for meaning, resulted in her fulfilling her purpose in life.
- The Apostle Paul started out as a Christian murderer, completely abusing his purpose in life. After an encounter with Christ, he became one of the most passionate defenders of Christ and the Christian faith writing most of the New Testament.

Where purpose is not known, abuse is inevitable.

Can you see any similarities with your own life? Is there something you currently hate like the Apostle Paul but it is your purpose in life? Are you rebelling against society like the "woman at the well" when your purpose is to be the answer to society?

You must understand that mishaps, mistakes and misunderstanding will never negate your purpose. Your purpose was tailor made for you and to your specifications. It does not matter what mistakes you have made, your purpose will not be taken away from you. Your past does not matter; you can still fulfill your purpose. If murderers, prostitutes and fornicators in the Bible can fulfill their purpose, then what can stop you from fulfilling yours?

The benefits of living on purpose

When you discover your purpose, it will cause you to:

- Reduce wasteful activities, which do not serve your purpose.
- Focus on what you want and automatically eliminate what you don't want.
- Become bold and courageous on route to overcoming obstacles.
- Network and initiate relationships with like-minded people.
- Be aware and protect your own uniqueness.
- Recognise that some things take time and persistently pursue them.
- Seek and take counsel from others.
- Dispel fear, intimidation and jealousy of others.
- Focus on the good in others.
- Recognise that others have information you don't, and choose to work with them.
- Obtain a mentor above you, and mentor those under you.

- Find a greater cause beyond yourself.
- Know your limitations.
- Create and inspire loyalty from friends.
- Attract opposition, which fuels your cause in life.
- Know your life was meant to benefit others.
- Be resourceful and relentless in not accepting no for an answer.
- Live a fulfilling life.
- Build integrity, and a good name with people.

You must know your purpose in life. Do you want to be:

- The best mother or father to your children?
- An inspiring public speaker that changes lives?
- A musician or actor who touches the emotions of others?
- Someone who cares for the hurting by giving them hope?
- An outstanding employee offering value to your employer?
- A skilful footballer that is a joy to watch?

Helice Briges said, "I'm not here just to make a living; I'm here to make a difference." Whose life will you impact? To whom will you make a difference? What is the difference you will make?

Hints to help you discover your purpose

To move your life from stop to start, it is critical to know your purpose. If you don't know it, consider the following questions:

- What natural gifts and abilities do you have?
- What is it that you are good at?
- What is it that energises you?
- What is it that you love?
- What are you passionate about?

- What is it that you hate? Maybe you were born to solve it?
- What do you consider the ideal role for you?

You must:

- Know your purpose.
- Plan your life around your purpose.
- Work your purpose.

This is the only way you will accomplish your purpose in life.

Purpose will always be calling you back on track if you are blown off course. Whatever the challenge you are going through right now, your purpose is a cause worth fighting for.

Without a purpose, you will be like a Frisbee in a hurricane, being tossed to and fro whichever way the wind blows. Stuff happens but don't allow the stuff of life to cause you to abort your purpose.

Our life lesson from the Japanese Carp fish

The Japanese Carp has unlimited growth. When you put the fish in a small bowl, it only grows to the size of the bowl and stop. The larger the bowl, the more it grows. It was made for maximum growth, but it allows the surroundings to stunt its growth.

It is the same with people; you can limit yourself based on your perception of your world. But once you know your purpose you can remove the limits from yourself, and unlimited growth will start to be fulfilled in your life. In other words, the more we upgrade our thinking in line with our purpose, the more we are likely to achieve it.

You can take a piece of paper and transform it into toilet paper and limit its value, or you can take that same paper and turn it in a hundred-dollar bill. The more the material is formed and developed, the more it grows in value.

It is the same with people. Are you settling for less when you were purposed for more?

Unstoppable purpose

As I write this book, Nelson Mandela is in the hospital and has celebrated his 95th birthday. He was confined to prison for 26 of those years because he was outspoken about apartheid. During this time, his purpose in life must have been really tested, and his hope for tomorrow challenged.

It is a tribute to his persistence, determination and belief in his purpose that he ultimately triumphed and went on to be elected to the highest office in his country.

Obstacles are part of the course of life, and you must find a way around them and become unstoppable. Obstacles are not there to break you but to make you better, stronger and bolder. Prime Minister Nelson Mandela made the following statements in his inaugural speech:

> *Our deepest fear is not that we are inadequate. Our deepest fear is that we are powerful beyond measure. It is our light not our darkness that frightens us.*
>
> *We ask ourselves, who am I to be brilliant, gorgeous, talented and fabulous? Who are we not to be?*
>
> *You are a child of God. Your playing small doesn't serve this world.*
>
> *There is nothing enlightened about shrinking so that other people won't feel insecure around you. We were born to make manifest the glory of God that is within us. It is not just in some of us; it is in everyone.*
>
> *And as we let our light shine, we unconsciously give other people permission to do the same.*

> *As we are liberated from our own fears, our presence automatically liberates others.*
>
> Source: A return to love by Marianne Williamson
> (as quoted by Nelson Mandela in his inaugural speech.)

This is a man who knew why he was born. He used the obstacles of life as a vehicle to keep him focused on his purpose in life. He made no excuses but took 100% responsibility for himself. In other words, he had learned self-mastery in the midst of a crisis and the crisis could not stop him, instead it propelled him to his destiny.

I would encourage you to write out your purpose in life, put it in your phone and read it at least three times per day. Develop a "purpose wall" and gather empowering pictures that will propel you to accomplish your purpose in life. On my "purpose wall" I have pictures of the crowds of people that I will impact and words saying "thank you for making a difference". I have the faces of men and women I would like to meet at my public speaking events. Look at the wall every day and picture yourself in it. Make it your preview of your forthcoming attraction. What you look at longest will become strongest in your life. What have you been looking at lately?

Benjamin Disraeli says, "A consistent man believes in destiny, a capricious man in chance". Let's be consistent in the steps we take on the road to fulfill our purpose in life.

Don't call time on your purpose; it's not over till your final breath.

Points to ponder and act upon before you leave this section.

1. *What problems do you love to solve?*

   ---

2. *If you could do anything in the world, what would it be?*

   ---

3. *What interests you?*

   ---

4. *What kind of books do you like to read, or what do you listen to in your free time?*

   ---

5. *What is it that you can do without much effort, but others struggle to do?*

   ---

6. Meditate on the above answers and the previous chapter, and write out what you consider to be your purpose in life.

   ----

7. Start to create a dream wall with at least 10 pictures which represent your purpose in life.

CHAPTER FOUR

I was Just Thinking

The empires of the future are the empires of the mind. -Winston Churchill

As a man thinks in his heart so is he. -Proverbs 23:7

How the unseen influences the seen

Many times what we see with the naked eye is a person's behaviour. That behaviour is driven by a number of unseen forces which we will examine more closely. If we see someone behaving badly, the point to remember is that the seen world is driven by the unseen. The bad behaviour is happening for a reason. For every cause, there is an effect; and for every action, there is an equal and opposite reaction.

Thoughts are a series of words; a dialogue that exists in the mind and is invisible, but is seen in the visible world through what we do, (i.e. our behaviours). It is not by coincidence or accident that we get what we are thinking about, whether it is good or bad.

If you are thinking negative thoughts, you exhibit negative behaviours, and if you are thinking positive thoughts, you will exhibit positive behaviours. In order to shift your life from stuck to start, you have to shift what you are thinking about. If you are thinking about the past, you will continually experience the emotions of the past repeatedly, whilst the present and future passes you by.

You can get into the groove of living in the past and not the future. This groove can take you straight to the grave, which is why people say the richest place on earth is the graveyard because it is full of unfulfilled dreams. What you think about determines what is attracted into your life.

The universe at large doesn't recognise whether your thoughts are positive or negative. The universe only recognises what we focus on and magnetises it to us. Malvin D. Saunders said that this is known as the "Law of Attraction," and it works even if we ignore it.

The past does not equal the future

Psychologists say that by the age of two, 50% of what we believe about ourselves has already been formed; by age six it's 60%, and by age eight, it's 80%. Isn't that sad to live the rest of our life by something that was perceived at age eight? Isn't that crazy?

As we grow, we realise we have our limits, but don't be your own limitation. Sir Edmund Hillary, the first person to reach the summit of Mount Everest said, "It is not the mountain we conquered, but ourselves." In other words, they took the limits off themselves and did what others said could not be done.

When Roger Bannister broke the four-minute mile, it opened the door for others to think this was possible. Within days, others who first thought it was impossible, ran a sub-four-minute mile. Why? They were previously limited by their thinking, but now realized it was possible. Now we have school kids breaking the four-minute mile.

As you think, so shall it be

Scientists tell us that our thoughts can create a bio-chemical response in our body, so our thoughts become our experience, which can mimic a reality that has not even happened. This means, for example, that you can think about a death that has not happened, and you can manifest the entire emotional trauma in your body as if the person actually died. Your thoughts can manifest the reality of an event that has not even occurred. Thoughts are powerful!

Now get ready - the opposite is equally true. If a sad event has occurred, it is only natural to acknowledge and experience the reality of it. However, to replay that sad event repeatedly in your mind is to experience the pain, hurt and disappointment over and over and over again. Even though the event occurred some five, ten or more years earlier.

The replaying of that event, like a broken record in the mind, makes it a present-day reality even when it may have occurred decades ago. Have you ever met someone who told you a sad story, and you asked them when did it happen? To your surprise, it happened a long time ago, but it sounds like it happened yesterday.

My brother is the opposite, he tells so many funny stories you would think they all happened yesterday, but they happened years ago. I have never seen him sad because his past funny stories are his present-day realities. Where your attention goes, your energy flows.

Now that you know this, you have a better understanding as to why you may have become stuck, or put on "pause."

In the previous chapter, you have determined what you would like to be in life i.e. what you want to work towards and accomplish with the rest of your life. Now you will have to shift from focusing on the past pain, hurts, failures, fears, and upsets, and make your future so bright that you have no choice but to live there now.

Now, it's time to look at yourself and examine your thoughts about past events. This will help you begin to turn the ship around, against the tide of the past, and point it in the direction of your choosing instead of allowing it to drift at sea.

You are the captain of your ship; you are responsible for your destination. You can direct your life from the depths of pain to take charge and exhibit your power over adverse circumstances.

Life is about overcoming obstacles, hindrances, painful experiences, and being a better person as a result of it. Crisis will come to us all at some time in our lives. How you deal with it, is determined by how and what you think.

To begin the process, you must start to think about what you are thinking about. Whatever cards life has dealt you, take them, play your best with them, and turn the game in your favour.

If I should ask you what a depressed person looks like, you might describe the position of the head, the frown on the face, the breathing and general countenance, the confused speech. But, how did you come to that conclusion? You did it by thinking about a depressed person. The reality is that what you think about the longest will become the strongest in your life.

Thoughts, focus, or beliefs play a key role in deciding how we feel. Look back in your life at all the times you were happy or sad, it was driven by your thoughts, focus, beliefs about sometime that had happened. You may not be able to alter the wind, but you can adjust the sails.

Manage your thoughts

I mentioned how I was stuck in a rut for a while when my Gran died. I kept thinking, time and time again, that I didn't get to say good-bye, and how death can be so cruel. This thought became the entirety of my focus. I thought about her absence from my life and not hearing her warm voice and laughter again.

The more this became my focus, the more negative I became, and the worst I felt psychologically and physically. I stopped socializing, stopped going to the gym for one, two, then three months. I started overeating and things went from bad to worse.

I told myself I was okay, but my self-image and confidence waned as I tried to come to terms with her absence from my life. Sounds familiar! I knew she had gone to a better place, free from pain, and that I had faith that we would meet again someday in the future, but that did not stop the pain of her absence from my life[vii]. The battle was in my mind, and the reality of her absence had slapped me in the face.

One day, I found myself thinking about the good times I shared with my Gran, and some of the funny stories she told me. I found myself focusing on the values she imparted in my life, and how much richer my life had become because of her. I started smiling to myself and being thankful that I was blessed with such a wonderful Gran.

Guess what? I started to feel better and better, second by second, minute by minute, and hour by hour. What happened? I had switched my focus from that which was negative and hindered me to that which was positive and empowered me. When I switched my thoughts, it felt like life returned to my body.

I had a different perspective on things and I no longer felt stuck, but started to take one small step towards regaining my equilibrium.

When I switched my thoughts to the memory of everything that was good and positive, I started to turn the ship in the direction I wanted to travel in. I started to feel less pain and more personal power.

One of my favourite expressions became, "if it's to be, it's up to me." I wrote this out on sticky paper and put it everywhere; in the house, on my phone, and on my the desk. I wrote a long list of all the happy memories of my Gran, which replaced the loss and absence I felt. As a man thinks in his heart so is he, and as I started to think more positively, so I became.

Someone once said that optimists are right; so are pessimists! Which one are you, or which one will be become?

Think your way out

When I was very helpful to a friend who then turned on me, I had to find a way to turn off the disappointment and despair and turn on my personal power. By activating your personal power, you are no longer a victim but a victor.

That experience was extremely humbling. I had made many sacrifices and spent a lot of money helping others to turn their situation around, but they turned on me instead. I was ostracized, criticised and stigmatised; it was a painful place, when close friends of yesterday turned into enemies of today. I was very saddened, depressed, and became stuck in a rut but it was only for a season. I felt the disappointment because I spent too much time thinking about the past, instead of the future.

I had to tell myself that I was not born with this problem, and that every problem has a solution and an expiration date. This is not an overnight fix. It was a process of self-examination and challenging my own thoughts until I found a solution to my own negative thinking.

This is a Biblical concept, and if you can grasp it, it will change your life. The Bible says that whatever is true, whatever is honourable, whatever is fair, whatever is pure, whatever is acceptable, whatever is commendable, if there is anything of excellence, and if there is anything praiseworthy keep thinking about these things. I started to think about what I could learn from this. How could I use adversity and disappointment to build my character and make me a better person?

If you look for the good in any bad situation, you will find it. My belief is that no experience, is ever a wasted experience.

In my heart, I knew that if I got bitter, I would have given away my personal power. I activated my personal power and continued showing love, even when it was painful – by this I would be demonstrating true power! It was very difficult. I had to take it step-by-step. When you end up shouting and quarreling and wanting to tell your side of the story, realise you are being a puppet on a string. Anytime you react or respond to the negativity of others, you have given away your personal power. You are no longer in control - they are. You have to think about how you can turn things around so that it works for you. You have to think your way out of the box you are in. If the house is on fire, you think about where the exit is, so you can exit the building calmly without tripping and needing to be rescued. You must use your positive thoughts to direct your path out of the current situation.

Good positive thinking

How I felt was a direct result of my thoughts. I was busy thinking about what other people might be thinking. I was thinking of the loss and the feeling of nothingness. In my despair, I remember thinking I would never help another person again. But at the same time I consoled myself by saying "not because it went wrong, doesn't mean I was wrong to help." When this thought kept recurring, one of the first things I did was to find the less fortunate in society and help them. I was determined that the pain of my misfortune would not dampen my compassion for others. You should not change your theology because of a tragedy. Compassion is higher-level thinking and higher-level living.

Albert Einstein said, "You can't solve problems by using the same kind of thinking you used when you created them." In other words, you have to go to another level in your thinking and in your doing.

The Bible says to think about the things that are true, honest, just, pure, lovely and of a good report.[viii]

I cannot determine the wind, but I can always adjust the sails. When I was going off course, I had to stop thinking about all the externals, i.e. what others are saying and focus on what I know to be the truth. I have learnt that it is not what people say about you that is painful – it is what you are saying to yourself about what they said, that causes pain and the hurt.

Think about that and see if it that resonates with you. The solution is to ensure you are not being used as a trash dump for negative reports.

You may have to delete some numbers from your phone and stop some callers from reaching your ears, so that you can make progress with your life. It might be hard initially, but it will pay you dividends in the long run.

For the friends who exited my life, I went back into my memory store and recalled all the joy I felt from being able to help those who needed help. I found some treasured memories. I recalled the chats, laughter, friendships, stories, funny incidents and joy we all shared. For each person, I made a handwritten note of something I really liked about him or her and focused on that every day. I recalled how my life was enriched because of these encounters and memories; it wasn't all negative, there was much good.

If you look for the good in a bad situation you will find it. I started to think good things about the people who disappointed me, and the good times we previously shared. I was thankful and grateful to have had such unique and amazing people in my life. I was thankful because they helped to build and shape my character and helped me to identify and use my personal power. I love to laugh and so recalled some of the funny things each person had done.

Even in the midst of pain, I found things to laugh about. Now that's power! Every day, I had to read the list of positives that I had written about each person. I chose to recall and laugh about the funny stories, until day-by-day the pain subsided. Through right thinking it all turned around for good.

I was very deliberate in keeping these lighter moments before my eyes and in my mind daily. I had to take time every day, to replace the negativity with the good, the true, the honest, the pure and the lovely thoughts.

Did I turn it around immediately? No, I did not. If you are driving a big lorry, you don't wait until you reach a corner to turn the lorry. It's a process and you build up to turn the lorry without hitting the curb. When I was learning this process of transforming from pain into power, I hit the curb many times. But, I kept on driving until I could turn without hitting the curb.

It's the same with emotional pain. It's a deliberate and intentional process of turning the pain of the negative into the power of the positive. The more you look for the good in the pain, the more you will find power in the process.

We all have the power to think: as we think, so shall we become. You should not allow personal pain to defeat you. Defeat it by the power of your thoughts and words. Always think about what you are thinking about. If you don't like how you feel, do a check-up from the neck up. Think about what you are thinking about, that will reveal why you feel the way you do.

If you change your thinking you will change your feeling. If you change your feeling you can change your world. In a nutshell, I am saying if you change your invisible words you will change your visible world.

You may have made a mistake, that doesn't mean that you are a mistake. If someone has died, it doesn't mean that you will never get over it. Because you were made redundant, does not mean you'll never work again.

Many people have pursued their passion after being made redundant and have gone on to brighter futures. I am one of them!

Many people have recovered from bereavement and gone on to live a fulfilled life. I am one of them!

Do you know that despite the pain of the past you can live and love and laugh again? I certainly do.

It's possible, but it all comes down to what you decide to think about. You don't have to accept the labels people place on you. Within you is the power to reject every negative label. Define your own label, and your own self-image. You must assure yourself about who you know you are on a daily basis. Use this to counter every false label people want to place on you. When you know who you are, their label of you will not affect you. Despite their rhetoric, be determined to become everything God made you to be. They could not stop Jesus or his disciples; be determined that they will not stop you.

Learning the lessons from the life of Job

No past, present, or future problem can stop the man or woman who has definiteness of purpose and lines up their thoughts with their purpose.

Justin Bieber said his all-time hero is Job. Job is a man in the Bible, who had everything; a wonderful and beautiful family, big house, lots of cattle and servants. One day, Job lost everything except his wife! His friends were not supportive, they criticised, ostracized and accused him of all evildoings, and tried to explain why he was suffering. Put yourself in Job's situation and imagine losing your family, house, job and cars. Only you and your spouse remain. Well, this story gets worse. Job's wife went one step further by encouraging Job to curse God and then die. She preferred death rather than face the pain of loss and the process of turning it into power.

Job was a very wise man, and he did not do as his wife requested. Job endured this ordeal for nine long and laborious months. He did not listen to the accusations of this wife or friends, but maintained his integrity.

It was a testing and humbling time in Job's life. Job remained true to himself whilst he was in crisis, and rejected all the labels from his wife and friends. He did not curse God. He did not blame anyone for his misfortune.

When you read the rest of Job's life story, in the end every loss was restored to him, and Job had "double for all his trouble." Job became prosperous in many ways, and in the end he had twice as many houses, children, cattle, servants, vineyards, etc. What a turnaround? Job went through the process and saw his pain turned into power.

Job's pain was for a reason. His story gives us hope that we might fall down, but the power is in the rising up. Just keep rising up one more time when you are knocked down. If Job had given up during his crisis, he would not have seen the reward for being an overcomer, a survivor. Only overcomers get the promotions and the rewards.

You must remind yourself that trouble comes to make and not break you. You may get knocked down on your journey but the power is in the getting back up.

In reading Job's life story, we see that shortly after he had lost his wealth and his children, he confessed that what he feared the most came to him. This tells us that Job feared loss and focused his thoughts on loss. As a man thinks in his heart so is he. So Job told himself everyday "I don't want to suffer any loss." This was negative thinking. Job focused on the wrong thing, and it became his reality.

The moral to this story is to think or meditate about what you do want, not what you don't want. This is why Mother Theresa said she would never attend an anti-war rally, but she would attend a peace rally instead. Think about that! Are there any unwanted things in your life that your thoughts attracted?

Know who you are and reinforce it

From today you should focus on the truth about yourself. Who are you really? You must write some powerful statements, put them in your phone, in your car, and repeat them to yourself first thing in the morning, last thing at night and throughout the day. These "I am" statements must replace every negative word or statement you say to yourself and what others have said about you. I have written some below that I use daily, but you can devise your own. Every day say out aloud the following:

- I am an overcomer
- I am wise in all circumstances
- I am a person of greatness
- I am happy and joyful
- I am getting stronger and stronger and better and better everyday

- I am changing for the best
- I am a champion
- I am a possibility thinker
- I am a fighter
- I am a survivor
- I am healthy and strong
- I am courageous
- I am respectful, respected, and in control
- I am a leader
- I am lovely in every way
- I am in charge of my destiny
- I am inspirational
- I am power

You must find the words that work for you. Always keep the statements in the positive and allow them to be your focus, your beliefs, and your daily thoughts. From day one, you will notice a shift, a lifting of the intensity of the pain you carry, and a positivity that is the returning of your power. Try it and see.

You must always remember that you have the power of choice. You have made a choice about your destiny and the new you. You have made a choice to refocus your thinking about the past, to look for the good in every painful circumstance, and to use that good to power your future. You have made a choice to devise and repeat your positive and empowering "I am" statements to reinforce the person you really are inside.

Your thoughts should now be more positive and realigned to your purpose in life. If you are still reading, these are some of the choices you have made so far.

Congratulations on your journey; you are making real progress as you exercise your personal power!

The workbook has some practical steps to help reinforce the new person you are becoming in terms of character building and self-image. Remember that your thoughts align with what you have decided you want to achieve as your purpose in life. You have one lifetime to make a lasting impression, and the time to start is right now. New choices create new results. Remind yourself daily of your new choices:

- I choose to take charge of my life as from this day forth.
- I choose to be positive in every negative situation.
- I choose to enjoy life.
- I choose to be happy every day and in every way.
- I choose to be healed of the past.
- I choose to live and to feel alive.
- I choose to be fit and healthy.
- I choose to set a new standard for my life.
- I choose to listen, learn and understand.
- I choose to find the answer for every problem in my life.
- I choose a higher level of thinking in order to shape my life.

Life doesn't just happen to you; it's all about the choices you make. The choice is about your thinking, your destiny, your friends, who you choose to listen to, etc. All these can change based on your choice. It is said that the 10 most powerful words in the English language are, "If it is to be, it is up to me." Do you think this statement is true?

The power of thought is well displayed in the following verses of the poem Thinking by Walter D. Wintle:

> If you think you are beaten, you are
> If you think you dare not, you don't,
> If you like to win, but you think you can't
> It is almost certain you won't.

> If you think you'll lose, you're lost
> For out of the world we find,
> Success begins with a fellow's will
> It's all in the state of mind.
>
> If you think you are outclassed, you are
> You've got to think high to rise,
> You've got to be sure of yourself before
> You can ever win a prize.
>
> Life's battles don't always go
> To the stronger or faster man,
> But soon or late the man who wins
> Is the man WHO THINKS HE CAN!

Your everyday positive thoughts should be aligned with your future, your destiny, and that purpose you want to achieve. When your thoughts are future-based, the past pain is only remembered for the strength of character it contributed to you and to your purpose. This is why it is important to gain focus and control your thoughts of the future, which is laid before you, instead of the past which is behind you.

Peace Pilgrim said, "If you know how powerful your thoughts are, you will never think a negative thought."

Do you believe that? Well, let's take a closer look at how your beliefs affect your purpose.

Points to ponder and act upon before you leave this section.

1. What negative emotions do you feel every day that you do not want?

   ----

2. What thoughts are driving these negative emotions and why you must stop them today?

   ----

3. What emotion would you like to have every day?

   ----

4. What action will you take today to have the emotion you desire?

   ----

5. What thoughts do you need to have to achieve your purpose?

   ----

6. Create at least 12 "I am statements" and read these first thing in the morning, last thing at night, and at least one throughout the day.

   These will reinforce the positive thoughts you have chosen.

CHAPTER FIVE

I Believe

Every man believes that he has greater possibility. -Ralph Waldo Emerson.

If thou can believe, all things are possible to him who believes. -Mark 9:23

The power of your beliefs

In the midst of every problem is the solution. There has never been a problem where a solution cannot be found. Do you believe that? It's not the problem that breaks you; it's how you respond to it. Your response is driven by your thoughts and beliefs about what has happened. These beliefs can destabilise your ability to respond appropriately and move forward.

Belief is at a deeper level than thinking. Belief is regarded as a fact or as a guiding principle that provides meaning and direction as you journey through life. What you believe may not even be truth, but your belief of it makes it true to you. When you believe something is true, it becomes your reality and many times nothing can dissuade you from it.

It's like giving a placebo to a patient. Once they believe that this is the cure to their malady, guess what happens – it becomes as they believe, and they are cured. So, your belief becomes a choice that you have decided to make.

We can choose beliefs that limit us, or choose beliefs that empower us. Many times I have heard people say that they are being punished for something they did in a former life. Can you believe that people actually believe that stuff, and consequently, fall into depression with no hope of recovery? A belief can be negative or positive. A negative belief is self- centred and serves only your interests, whilst a positive belief is good and serves the greater good.

The secret in life is to pick beliefs that empower you towards success and achievement, and let go of the ones that hold you back.

Beliefs are the compass that we use to assist us in the achievement of our goals and empowers us to keep going forward in life to attain higher heights. When you change what you believe, you will change your behaviours and actions.

Studies have shown that beliefs are driven by:

- The environment in which we live and move in regularly.
- Results of the past.
- Events which have happened and left an indelible print in us.
- Knowledge that we have attained over the years.
- Thinking of the future and believing as if it's happening now.

I was born in the UK, raised in a little district in Jamaica, and I have been in the UK now for over thirty years. It's amusing at times, when I go back to Jamaica and speak to some of my friends. They genuinely believe that the entire world is just like their little district, because that's the environment they have been exposed to. They are influenced by the news and the negativity, and some have never left the neighbourhood.

Similarly, there are others who have left the neighbourhood with the mind- set that life is no better. So many leave the district and go to foreign shores and connected with people from their new neighbourhood who have the same beliefs. They only see difficulties and no opportunities because they are fuelled by their convictions, opinions and beliefs of the past. Could it be that your beliefs about past events have you stuck in a rut?

Others have travelled and been exposed to new ideas, concepts and different cultures and have realised that the world is their oyster, and that they have the power within to do all things. They are not limited by others, the only limit is based on what they choose to believe. They are driven by a conviction, opinion and belief of a future filled with endless possibilities.

Beliefs are so strong that what you believe about your purpose in life, will determine whether you succeed or fail.

Choose beliefs that empower what you want to achieve

I will never forget when I was 17 years old, I went to the doctors with shoulder pain. It was so bad that it would take me about 15 minutes to get out of bed. I could not lift my hand above my head nor put on a dress or a blouse. After a number of tests and an x-ray, I went back to see my doctor. I remember sitting there in his office and with a perplexed look on his face he said, "Well its bad news, it appears you have a degenerative bone defect in your shoulders, and you will have to take prescription drugs for the rest of your life to help with the pain." I looked at him as if he had lost his mind. I thought he was reading the wrong diagnosis to the wrong patient. I replied, "What?" He said, "It probably runs in your family." I told him that no one in my family had bone problems that I was aware of. The doctor gave me a prescription for a thirty-day supply of anti-inflammatory drugs, and he asked me to return in three weeks for an assessment. I remember as I walked away I said to myself, "I don't believe this, and I won't accept this."

I started my quest for knowledge about my condition; I just did not believe and could not accept having to take tablets for the rest of my life. I took the prescription for one week to help with pain management, whilst I searched the internet about degenerative bone issues. I started to read about the difference between acidic and alkaline foods, and that when the body is acidic, it draws nutriments from the bones. I realised that the solution was to change what I was eating and not to start taking tablets. At age 17, I stopped the tablets and started to eat more healthily. I started to feel the results within days, and within one month, the pain had gone. It has been nearly thirty year now and this health issue has never returned because I acted on what I believed. My belief turned my pain into power.

The morale of the story is that my belief about the situation resulted in the outcome I wanted. I am not encouraging anyone to do what I did. My response was purely a personal one, in that I believed the disease in the body was primarily triggered by something, which happened to be my high acidic diet. I also have a belief that in some cases, removing what I am putting into my mouth can eliminate the nature of the disease. As I believed it to be, so it was. Anton Chekhov said, "man is what he believes."

The making of a champion

Often, when you encounter relationship problems, particularly with close friends or co-workers, the root cause is jealousy. Once you know this, it gives you a different perspective on things, so you can look for the good that will work for you in every bad situation. The key is to look at every situation in terms of your desired outcome, and then take action to accomplish what you desire. If you desire to triumph over every negative situation, then you must do what champions do. You must have a plan of action, and work your plan by being persistent, diligent, and relentless until you get your desired outcome.

It is a sad fact of life, but not everyone wants you to succeed. Some people envy your progress and success and will try to knock you off your perch. You must be determined and resilient in the pursuit of your dream or your purpose in life. You can be shaken but not stirred. You might be down but never out. You may fall, but you will rise again. You might feel deflated but believe that you will bounce right back. Begin by talking positively to yourself.

In other words, you have to encourage yourself and not allow anything or anyone to rain on your parade.

In the Bible, just before David was finally crowned King of Israel, he plummeted into deep despair. This happened because he had left his family and had gone to war with men from his camp, but in his absence, the camp was raided and all the inhabitants were taken captive. David's men blamed him and wanted to stone him because their families were taken captive. David's family was also taken and he was also hurting, but because he was the leader they all turned on him. Can you imagine how you would feel in this situation? Imagine the depth of burden and sense of responsibility for others and for your own family. But, the Bible says that David encouraged himself[ix]. David sought the Lord who answered him, he rallied his men, pursued the raiders, and rescued their families and recovered everything that was stolen from them. Because David encouraged himself, he was able to deal with the situation in a way that resulted in a positive outcome. Will you do the same when faced with discouragement?

There are times when you can't look outwards for help, but you have to look inwards for strength. You have to come to the place where you believe that all you need is already within you. John Stuart Mill said, "One person with a belief is equal to a force of ninety-nine who have only interests." You have to believe in yourself even when others don't. This is your source of strength.

Quitters will never win

J Willard Marriott said, "Good timber does not grow with ease; the stronger the wind, the stronger the trees." You need opposition to build you up. No one becomes a champion until they overcome some adversity. You must switch your beliefs and see obstacles as opportunities for your greatness. Ask any great sportsman or woman, any politician or entrepreneur about their testimony on their route to greatness. You do need people to be against you. It's prove that you believe in yourself enough to make it, irrespective of the opposition you face. If you quit when the going gets tough, you will never win.

The opposition exists for you to build new and empowering beliefs which will impact your behavior. This will help you to be an overcomer and more than a conqueror. Someone wrote a book entitled "Believe in the God who believes in you." It's reassuring to know that God believes in you, and he knows that you are more than able to overcome any obstacles that come your way. The Bible confirms that He will never allow more to come to you than you can handle.

So, when problems come your way, see it as a compliment that it came to you because you are more than able to survive and thrive in spite of it. If we can just believe, all things are possible.

Normal Vincent Peale reminded us to "Believe in yourself." You must have faith in your abilities. Without a humble but reasonable confidence in your God given power it's hard to be successful or happy. Otherwise, you look for everything outside when the power to turn the troubles of life around is already inside you.

How beliefs impact your purpose

The future is in your hands. Everything that it takes for you to fulfil your purpose in life is already within you. It is not in your friends, family or employer, but in you.

- It is in you to overcome.
- It is in you to prevail.
- It is in you to prosper.
- It is in you to be victorious.
- It is in you to come out on top.
- It is in you to win.
- It is in you to turn your pain into power.

It all depends on what you believe. Nelson Mandela had such a belief system that even when the guards buried him up to his neck, and urinated on his head, he held firm to his belief that all men were born equal.

Whilst in captivity, he earned a Bachelor of Law degree from the University of London, and became a mentor to fellow prisoners.

Whilst in captivity, he started making progress towards his destiny. This is what Joseph also did. Nelson Mandela didn't choose disempowering, self-centred limiting beliefs; he had found his purpose, which was bigger than himself. It was a cause that was worth laying aside personal motives, so every man, woman, boy, and girl would come to the realization that all were born equal.

Now, you have a better understanding of why people are stuck in a rut, unable to get out. Their thoughts and beliefs do not align with where they are going. Many people want to be financially independent, but believe they are doomed to being broke, busted and disgusted because of the recession. This is a flawed belief system. It is not conducive to what they want, and so they remain broke, and blame it on the global recession.

In reality, their belief in the recession is greater than their belief in their own financial independence. Similarly, many believe that the past is equal to the future. They want a brighter future, but get stuck in the past due to limiting beliefs. It is what we think and believe that will propel us into taking consistent action to fulfil our destiny or purpose in life.

Faith comes by hearing - be careful what you hear

Whatever the outcome you can see in your life, you should check to verify if that is what you believed. Many times you are the creator of that outcome, based on your thoughts and beliefs.

When I told a friend that I had malaria, she proceeded to tell me of all the persons she knew who died from malaria! I did not want to hear that. My only response was to delete her number from my phone because I wanted to live and not die.

You may think this was harsh, but it was the right thing to do. Don't allow people to talk you into death, depression and despair. Faith comes by hearing, so eliminate negative voices from your ears so you can live.

I am glad to say, I am not a ghost writer, I am still here today, alive and well.

Your current circumstance is a direct result of your belief system. If your thoughts become dominated by the belief of abundance, equality, prosperity, joy, health, growth and maximum potential, (which are positive beliefs towards your desired end), then this will gravitate towards you. As you focus on your beliefs, doors and opportunities will begin to open for you. This choice you have to make is between an empowering belief, and a limiting belief.

Take back your power

You may have now realised that you gave your personal power away to wrong beliefs. Now it's time to turn it around and take it back. You may know the story of this young woman who was born through a lineage of incest. This topic is very taboo and in today's world, people would be shunned because of it.

This young lady's name was Ruth, and she became an unexpected widow. Ruth was an outcast because of her background, but when her husband died, she decided to leave town and stay close to her mother-in-law whose name was Naomi. Naomi was also a widow. Ruth, with such an adverse background, could have believed that she was a "nobody," a "non-achiever" and that nothing good would become of her life.

As the two women journeyed together, Naomi became a mentor to Ruth, and in the succeeding months, Ruth met and married a man named Boaz. Boaz was well-established and in today's age would be classed as a millionaire. This same Ruth became the great-grandmother of King David, and an ancestor in the lineage of the Messiah. Her belief in who she was changed her destiny. We can see that Ruth had no control over the circumstances of her birth. However, she did not allow that negative "label" to stick to her nor to impact her belief about who she was.

She could not change her past, but she had a strong belief about who she was, which impacted her future. She believed in herself and allowed the issues and sorrow of the past to pass by. Ruth firmly believed that she was not a mistake, she was not illegitimate, nor was she an accident. But, she was born on purpose for a purpose. Your beliefs make all the difference to your destiny.

We all have the freedom of choice about what to believe. Our beliefs will significantly impact how we behave. Tony Robbins says, "I've come to believe that all my past failure and frustration were actually laying the foundation for the understandings that have created the new level of living I now enjoy." Can you say the same thing – I can.

Today is the day to take back your personal power. Today is the day to choose empowering beliefs to facilitate your journey to destiny. Let's continue and examine the impact of beliefs on our emotions.

Points to ponder and act upon before you leave this section.

1. What limiting beliefs do you have about yourself and your purpose?

   ----

2. Why or what caused those limiting beliefs?

   ----

3. In the light of what you have read, how can you challenge and demolish those limiting beliefs?

   ----

4. What empowering beliefs do you need to have to achieve your purpose?

   ----

5. What will you do each day to reinforce your positive beliefs?

   ----

6. Write out your new beliefs and commit to read them aloud at least three times per day, morning, noon and night.

CHAPTER SIX

Feeling Emotions

Take control of your consistent emotions and begin to consciously and deliberately reshape your daily experience of life.
-Tony Robbins

I discovered I always have choices and sometimes it's only a choice of attitude. -Unknown

The invisible is always made visible

Emotion is something that can be seen by the naked eye. It is driven by what cannot be seen, i.e. our thoughts and beliefs. In other words, the invisible world of thoughts and beliefs results in the visible world of our emotions.

Thoughts and beliefs, which drive negative emotions, are usually associated with an underlying event. This event could be death, redundancy, unfair treatment or criticism, to name a few. The visible results of negative emotions can be seen in the expression of anger, annoyance, depression, disappointment, sadness, distrust, contempt, and the like.

If these emotions continue to fester, they can quickly become debilitating to your health. On the contrary, thoughts and beliefs which drive positive emotions are associated with underlying events such as victory, progress, success, achievement, accomplishment to name a few. This can lead to positive emotions such as joy, trust, zeal, satisfaction, love, courage, contentment, gratitude, excitement, affection and the like. It is said that the quality of your life is the quality of the emotions you constantly experience and exhibit.

The word *emotion* means to move away from. In other words, you move from a place of what is balanced, to a place of extremes.

It also means a complex, usually strong subjective response, involving physiological changes, as a preparation for action. The physiological changes include things like shallow breathing, clenching teeth, upset stomach, wrinkled forehead, aggressive tone of voice, crying spells, to name a few. We have all experienced some of these, and oftentimes refer to these as life.

One day you are happy, and the next you are sad. Today you are up and tomorrow you are down. These inconsistent variations of our emotions are not conducive to long term joy, peace and contentment, as it disables the power within you to make your dreams a reality. When you consistently experience such extremes, it in an indication that you are out of balance.

The necessity of self control

In handling your emotions, you have to be honest with yourself. If you are led by negative emotions, this can be damaging to you and all who are around you. If you consistently act without thinking, always having to apologise, the consequences of such emotions can be devastating. You have to transition to a place where you start to manage and control you^x. If you try to control people and circumstances, you will head for the road call "self-destruction," which will always be under construction.

Trying to control everything will lead to a life of perpetual frustration as people and circumstances refuse to live up to your expectation. Until you can control yourself, you won't be able to have mastery over your emotions, your destiny or the circumstances around you. If you refuse to control your emotions, you will be pushed from pillar to post, blaming situations, circumstances and people for the misery you feel within.

The truth is, you have to take 100% responsibility for what you are feeling now and what or how you want to feel. Life may not have dealt you the perfect pack of cards, but if you play your cards right, you can still win.

Think about the AA prayer, and try to apply the principles to your life. The prayer goes like this:

> God grant me the serenity;
> To accept the things I cannot change;
> Courage to change the things I can;
> And wisdom to know the difference.

Change the way you see things

It takes courage to understand that you cannot change people, you cannot change what has happened, but you can only change your perception of what has happened.

It is not what happens to you but how you respond to it that really matters. In addressing your negative emotions, you will need to identify:

- What negative emotions from your past, have you suppressed?
- If you can associate any ailments of illnesses in your body with those emotions.
- Whether you have tried to medicate an emotion that you refuse to confront?
- How can you challenge your emotions with truth?
- How you can measure the intensity of your emotions daily and reduce them?

I refer to these in depth within the workbook. The analysis will help you to realise that circumstances or situations are not limiting you, but you are limiting yourself. You have to turn the spotlight on you. In other words, you have to look inward and fully understand what you are feeling now and create an empowering belief that will begin to turn your emotions from negative to positive.

The source of your power lies within you. You have what it takes to turn your live around from bad to good and from pain to power.

To shift your life let bygone be "bye" and "gone"

The past will only equal your future if you live there, so you must find a way to learn the lessons from the past and use them to your advantage in the future. It is not unusual to find that people, who have been hurt badly in the past, have succumbed to building walls of defence around them. No one can penetrate that wall, no one can enter in and nothing comes out.

This is a defence mechanism to prevent them from being hurt again. They can easily become cold and callous on the inside, often unaware of the hurt of others, and they then tend to be judgmental and critical of the mistakes of others.

With my history of hurts and pain, I was this person. Still, such an emotionless person can be turned around to one that is compassionate and sensitive to the needs of others. Such a person can turn their pain to power by confronting their emotions and making a decision to let go of the past. You have to say "bye and be-gone" to the past so you can start a new chapter in your life.

Know what's driving you.

You can now begin to see that emotions drive everything. Whether you laugh or cry, hate or love, be at war or at peace; it's all about what you feel. No one acts without the feeling that they have to do something. In other words, the meaning I give to anything at the time, drives my emotions. Our emotions cause us to act out what we feel.

As I write this book, I am driven by the positive emotion of joy, knowing that this book will turn around the lives of many, from a place of pain to a place of power. Had it not been for the many emotional ups and downs in my own life, I would not have discovered that the power was within to change for good. By managing my emotion, I was no longer stuck in the pain of past events, but transitioned to have an empowering and fulfilling future.

To transition your negative emotions, which are displayed on the outside, you have to address the twins of thoughts and beliefs. If you are not feeling the way you would like to, it is an indication that something within needs to change.

Confront your emotions and be healed

Our thoughts and beliefs drive emotions. Positive and healthy emotions are driven by positive healthy thoughts and beliefs. While negative unhealthy emotions are driven by negative unhealthy thoughts and beliefs. If you are not getting the desired emotions, then you have to do a check-up from the neck up on your thoughts and beliefs.

When my Gran died, I could not escape the current-day reality of her absence from my life. I had not encountered this level of bereavement before, and I felt an emptiness that I thought would last forever. I also was suffering from feelings of guilt because I had promised her that I call her the day before she died, which I didn't.

You must challenge the things you believe when a crisis hits you. I found myself saying, "Maybe, just maybe, if I had called her yesterday, she would be alive today." Can you image the magnitude of the emotional guilt and responsibility upon my shoulders for believing such a lie?

Looking back now, it seems inconceivable that I swallowed that belief and lived in self-pity because of it.

You can blame yourself for so many things when you are hit by a crisis or by bad news. If you leave this kind of belief unchallenged, it will do its job and consume you. So, you must question and challenge your thoughts and beliefs, which affects you negatively.

I had weeks where I blamed myself and I experienced the negative emotions of depression, grief, and guilt. It took me some time to start to challenge my "fuzzy" logic.

Today, I miss my Grans' presence in my life, but each day the grief gets lighter and lighter. I noticed that whenever I would think about the time I spent with my Gran, and recalled her many funny stories and jokes, my whole physiology changed. I would breathe better, I would smile and be at peace. But, whenever my thoughts and beliefs were negative, so were my emotions.

Let me explain. The transformation of my negative emotions became a process of monitoring and adjusting my belief system, by looking at all the good until my emotions aligned with my new empowering beliefs.

I remembered some of the conversations I had with my Gran in the months and weeks before she died, and realised that each conversation was a preparation for her departure. It was the separation, by distance that made our conversations more lasting and memorable. I looked back over my life and believed that in every contact I had with my Gran, she was mentoring me for my future.

Now, that's an empowering and liberating belief. It was when I got to this level of thinking and believing that I started to switch from pain to power in my emotions.

Look for the good in every bad situation

Similarly, when I was made redundant during a period of ill health, I experienced worry, dread, and frustration, to name a few. These emotions were triggered by the fact that I believed my employer was wrong. I started to believe I might never work again. My belief system had not empowered me to think outside the box and to achieve greater things; it was quite the opposite. The more negative my thoughts and beliefs, the worst my illness became.

I had to challenge my beliefs with truth. The truth of the situation was that I was signed off on long-term illness having contracted malaria. At the time, I was the director of a company with about twenty-two staff and no guaranteed income for the business beyond one year. The business could not survive without new sources of capital and leadership; none of which I could provide from a sick bed.

One day, I asked myself some soul searching questions like, "if the tables were turned, Rose, what would you do?" Guess what, I came to the same conclusion as my boss did. I concluded that I would offer a golden good-bye, and bring in someone new to provide the vision, leadership and security that staff needed. My employer was not wrong but was spot on. Once I found the good in this bad situation, my emotions stated to realign with the new truth.

However, before this turnaround happened, I had wasted many days being in disgust, depression and despair, until I looked at the issue from a totally different perspective.

Until I started to have empowering beliefs about redundancy and life after redundancy, I could not move forward.

Thereafter, I started to dream of a new level of freedom, of starting my own business, of working when I wanted to work and of being able to pursue other dreams I had put on hold.

I was switching from a victim to a victor mentality. Lies will cost you, but the truth will liberate you. You must choose which one you prefer.

The reality is, I did start my own company and worked the hours I wanted and pursued new hobbies, including writing this book. The moment I switched what I believed about redundancy, I felt liberated. My employer was no longer in control of my destiny but I was. I was in the driving seat on route to my destiny. I was emancipated from mental slavery.

From the moment I switched and took back my personal power, I felt positive emotions of contentment, gratitude, and peace. It was at the same time the malaria started to leave my body, and I started to feel humane again.

Why? Because I had chosen the invisible world of empowering thought and beliefs to drive the visible world of positive emotions of what I desired. You will know the truth, and the truth will set you free[xi]. I was free.

So many times we focus on a lie that keeps us stuck in time, but when we face the truth, positive movement begins in our life.

Lessons from the moulting eagles

Many times, as you travel along life's journey, you might meet people with whom you become great friends, but who may disappoint you tomorrow. When this happened to me, I found myself in a wilderness, a place of isolation. It was in this place that my healing and recovery started and I processed into power.

During this season, I felt it necessary to separate myself from friends who unknowingly were supporting my pain, and prolonging the negative emotions I felt, when what I really wanted was to feel joy, peace and to be healed.

You must know what you want and where you are going. Only then can you enlist the help of friends who want to see you healed and recovered to help you in the process. What you need during this season is not sympathy but compassion. Sympathy will hug you leave you the way you were found; whilst compassion will hug you and offer you help to become better than when you were found.

Anthony Robbins says "decisions decide destiny." Many times, in order for you to endure the race of life and be free, you have to be healed of your emotional wounds so that your strength can be restored. This is why injured soldiers don't go to fight at the front line. They are put in at the back away from harm, until they are healed. Only when they are fully restored are they allowed on the front line.

As I recalled the story of the injured soldiers, I remember learning about the eagles. Eagles are the most majestic birds in the sky, but at least once in their lifetime, they go through the moulting process. This is a depressing time for the eagles, as they begin to lose their feathers and beak, and their hunting claws start to alter. During this time, this most majestic bird that rules the sky will walk on the ground like a turkey because they have no strength at all to fly. The moulting eagles will remain in the valley as they become weaker. The weaker they become, the more their feathers are being depleted. As their vision weakens, they lose their ability to see clearly.

Due to the moulting process, calcium builds up on their beak; their heads become too heavy to be lifted up, and so they flop down. The eagle can lose its desire to eat or even to fulfil its natural instincts and hunt for food. These are pretty desperate times, and sometimes the moulting eagles turn on each other even unto death.

Sometimes the moulting eagles will choose a mountain range where the sun can shine directly on them, and they will lie on a rock and bathe in the sun for comfort. Some of the other "healthy" eagles will fly by and drop food to the ones going through this "moulting" stage.

Apparently, it's the older and not the younger eagles that will drop the food. You might ask why it is the older ones. This is because the older ones know what the moulting eagles are going through because they have been through it and survived.

The carrying of food acts as a reminder that help is available, that they must not give up, but go through the process. The younger eagles are usually unaware that their day will come. Some eagles eat and recover whilst others keel over and die. The truth is, if the eagles do not go through the moulting process, if they do not renew themselves, they will die anyway, so they must go through the process to live.

Will you go through the process? Will you lay low for a while until your strength is renewed like the eagles? Will you allow others to help you? Will you go through the process and live, not die?

What we have failed many times to understand is that the eagles may look weak, battered, tired, rejected and neglected on the outside during moulting, but the eagle's strength is being renewed on the inside. In other words, whilst the outside was perishing, the inside was being renewed daily[xii].

Many times we put more emphasis on what we can see, but the strength and the power is in what we cannot see. Like the moulting eagle, the seasons will present you with pain and pleasure, tears and joy, all at the same time.

When I was recovering from the hurt and disappointment of being shunned, I now look back and realise that my wilderness experience of being ignored, talked about, and being rejected was the best thing that could have happened to me. Many passed by with no nuggets of encouragement for me to feed on. But it was the Pastor, confidants, and matured mothers in the church that dropped nuggets of encouragement for me to feed on. I salute you and say thank you.

Others thought that because I was out of sight taking nourishment from the sun, I was finished. My head was down and low, but only for a while. My spirit was crushed to pieces, but it was only for a while. My purpose was unsure, but it was only for a while, and like the moulting eagle I felt like I wouldn't survive.

The feeling was only for a while. But in the fullness of time, there was a lifting of my head and a restoration of my battered soul. My purpose took on new wings, and my joy was revived.

My strength had been renewed, and my time had come to mount up on wings like an eagles, to run and not be weary, to walk and not faint[xiii]. The Bible tells us that if the enemies of Jesus had known Him, they would not have crucified Him[xiv]. What was meant to take you low is the very thing that will raise you high. Don't fear nor despair, the process is only for a season. Go through it, overcome the obstacles and transition into your power like the eagle.

Fortify your mind

During this season in my life, I started my days with positive self-talk, and scripted positive messages to read to myself throughout the day. I decided to speak good about myself, even if it was just to myself. Every morning I reminded myself that:

- There is greatness in me
- There is goodness in me
- There is love in me
- There is honesty and integrity in me
- There is great value in me
- There is uniqueness in me
- There is creativity in me
- There is a survivor in me
- There is a champion in me

This positive self-talk, based on what I discovered in the Bible, was to become my medicine, my image builder and soul repairer. You have to put yourself at the centre, because you are the only person you can control. You can only control yourself and your emotions. If you speak positively and passionately to yourself like this every day and believe it in your heart, something inside you will begin to shift. There will begin to be some movement, a turning of the negative to the positive, and a turning of pain into power.

Pay no attention to your critics

You have to transition to forget those things that are behind you and press ahead to achieve those things before you.[xv]

You must learn to discard the antics of your critics. Do not allow them to dictate your emotions. You must know that whatever they meant for your downfall; will turnaround and be your uprising. If you know this from the outset, you will exercise your personal power and channel it into fulfilling your purpose in life.

Your future is in your hands, you are in control of it; no one else is. You must know what you want, why you want it, and take steps to access it now. You must position yourself in the centre of what you want. You must stand there unshakable, unmovable and undeniable until you get what you have purposed.

You cannot stay in oblivion and obscurity forever. However, during this wilderness experience, there are a number of things, which you must address and settle within yourself so that you walk in power and not pain. These are in the headings below.

Do good to those who despise you

To do good to those who despise is a spiritual concept and a powerful tool. Let me explain how it works. About five months into my recovery period, I met some of the people who had disappointed me and weren't nice to me. You know what I did, I hugged and kissed and greeted them with the biggest smile and kindest of words.[xvi]

Inside, I still felt the hurt and the pain, but I found out that showing love to someone who expected you to show discord or indifference is a very disarming tool. Napoleon Hill wrote a book on "Outwitting the Devil," and this is exactly what you must do.

When I did this to a friend, it completely freaked her out, she avoided me like the plague. She went from a giant to a pygmy, she became confused, started walking in a different direction to avoid me.

Your heart is too small to plan bad things, plan good things instead even if you don't feel like it.

If you keep doing good things, good feeling will follow. The good feeling will not happen overnight, but you must do what is good, until your feelings align to what you do.

Forgive and live

In every situation that I have shared, I had to deal with the area of forgiveness in order to master my emotions. Forgiveness is not the absence of remembering what happened, but is remembering and choosing to smile about it, knowing that it was meant for bad, but it turned around for your good. Even if you can't see the good at present, choose to believe that you might be crying today but will be laughing tomorrow.

You don't have to be stuck and relive the hurt and pain of the past. Every time you rehearse it, you relive it, and you suffer it over and over again. The coward dies 1000 times, but the brave only once.

How many times will you pick at the scab and expect it to heal? Forgiveness heals the soul and releases you to laugh, love and live again. It brings you to a point where you must physically close the book to what happened in the past. Until you forgive and close that book, you are limited and restricted to opening a new book in your life.

There is a story where Jesus read in front of his severest critics, and then He closed the book. When Jesus closed the book in the physical, he opened himself up to a new dimension of life and never looked back. You will not make the progress you desire until you close the book on your past, and open yourself to embrace the possibilities and power of the future.

You cannot look back whilst looking forward at the same time. It's one or the other, so you have to choose. You have a purpose in life to fulfil. Like all good champions, you have to reflect and learn from the past, but use the past pain to become better and greater in the future. You have to allow the pain of the past to be your power for the future.

Just imagine if Anthony Robbins, David Beckham, or President Obama was sitting on your sofa right now. For all the mistakes and hardships they suffered in the past, they still became great. They became great household names, because they learned to forgive. The pain of what they suffered could not hold them back; it was a tool for their greatness. The people and circumstances of their lives were just there to launch them into their destiny.

You must know that when you don't forgive it ties up your emotions and restricts you from moving ahead. It keeps you as a prisoner whilst the offending party is walking free. You must release yourself from the grip of wanting and hoping that the offending person be punished. The best revenge you can take against those who hurt you is to forgive them and become everything you were created to be. To continue to blame others, is a poor excuse for not being everything you were created to be.

I will never forget when I had to take a BA flight and travel over 6000 miles to tell someone "I forgive you." This person had spoken negative, soul-destroying words in my life since I was young. I held onto those negative, crippling words from my youth to adulthood. The time had come to switch off the pain and switch on the power.

She had wronged me. Yet one day, I heard this conversation inside, saying, "isn't it time you go and say I'm sorry to Jane and take her a present." I could not believe it. Jane had wronged me and I was to apologise. Worse yet, I was to take her a present. You are kidding me!

The more I tried not to think about it, the more I heard the same message. I had so much conviction that I took a flight and travelled 6000 miles. I'll never forget the day that I was to go and visit Jane; I rehearsed and rehearsed three little words for nearly twelve months. The words were "I forgive you." Jane knew what she had done and said.

I woke up early in the morning, and the day seemed as quiet and as peaceful as monks in prayer. Within me was turmoil, dread, fear of this mammoth task that I had taken on. I could eat nothing, but tried to focus my mind to do what I travelled 6000 miles to accomplish.

Jane's house was not far away, but it felt like I had started a journey to Mars. I could feel the perspiration on my brow, as my heart quickened the closer I got to Jane's house. At one stage, I felt that I should do a U-turn and forget about the ridiculous idea. 6000 miles and now I wanted to turn around.

I persevered, knocked on Jane's door, and footsteps like the sound of Hercules approached the front door. A creaking door, like something from the living dead opened. As I stood there, I connected with the piercing almost evil eyes of Jane. Out of my mouth came, "Hi Jane, I brought you a present and just wanted you to know I forgive you". I could hear Jane was stuttering, and her mouth produced no words as I handed her the gift, turned and walked away.

WOW! At first I felt dreadful, but as I walked I felt a lifetime of burden lifted from me. The past had died, and the book had been closed. It was like a prisoner set free, a yoke was lifted from my shoulder, a choke hold was released from my throat. She meant it for evil, but it turned out for my good.

I became a new woman as joy came and filled my soul. Shortly afterward, I started to set out plans for my future. I came up with creative ideas and witty inventions. The change that had occurred meant the clutter had gone from my soul, and I was free to live again.

The turnaround came when I let go of the past, only then could I embrace the future. This is what you must do today. Don't wait another minute; don't allow another day to pass you by, do it today. Now is the time to forgive. I had to forgive my boss. I had to forgive my friends, and I had to forgive myself. Jane, who used to intimidate me, now avoids me. That was not my intention, but this is what happens when you turn your pain into power.

Max Lucado said "Man's greatest need is for forgiveness. This is why God sent a Saviour." If God has forgiven you, you can forgive anybody.

Know the truth - the truth will set you free

You shall know the truth, and the truth shall set you free. In the midst of emotional turmoil, assess if what you feel will serve you for the better.

If it does not, you must resist it, otherwise your life will remain miserable and unstable. Whatever emotional issues you have right now, you were not born with it. This means you have the power to change it.

Have you ever witnessed the birth of a baby and understand the stressful journey they travel to come into the world. It's a journey consisting of twists and turns from one world into another world, I hope you agree that by time the baby was born, the baby was:

- An overcomer.
- A survivor.
- A conqueror.
- A success story.
- A champion.
- A winner.
- A person of purpose.

This was how we all came into the world, already achieving the miraculous. So, when challenges come, even in the midst of working them through, remind yourself of whom you are at the core. You are not a failure; you are a success story. You are not a loser; you are a winner.

You must use the truth to reinforce the permanency of who you are at the source, overcoming every temporary situation that arises. You should not allow situations and circumstances to negate the truth of who you are at the centre of your core. What you continually confess, is what you will possess.

If you refuse to be truthful to yourself, you give your power over to lies. When I say truthful, I don't mean you should deny what happened. What I mean is that you should look for any areas in your life where you can improve and be a better person, and decide that irrespective of what has happened you will keep moving forwards. In essence, you should challenge and question your own thoughts and emotions with the truth.

This is what I mean about being truthful to you. Ask yourself, what good can come out of this pain I am going through right now? How can I become better and not bitter? How can I lead myself to a better future?

You cannot change what you do not confront. It's time to stop being driven by your emotions and begin to look for the truth in your problem. I have a work book which will help you to clarify this position.

When the man I was to marry married someone else, yes I hurt for a while. However, I told myself that he wasn't the one, and the one I was waiting for was still somewhere out there. Now that's a truth which empowered me. I didn't believe I had missed the boat, nor left on the shelf. And surely, 16 years later I was married to the one.

Imagine what could have happened if I had just sat at home and cried, got depressed and held a self-pity party. I would have told everyone about my sad, sorry story, and received their sympathy. My life would have been miserable; I would have been stuck in a rut. But, because I survived to live, laugh and love again, I have written this book to encourage others. You can find truth that empowers you, even in adverse situations.

When my Gran died, I had to tell myself that I would have hated her to be alive and be in and out of hospital with needles in her arm and such like; taking pills that might cure one problem but caused another.

What is the truth about your situation that will liberate you right now? When I was made redundant, I had to transition and encourage myself that the future was brighter than my past. So, after I recovered my health, I started my own consultancy business just under a decade ago, and I have never looked back. The alternative would have been to fall into depression, and repeat the same-old story time and time again. This is the recipe for a miserable existence.

What lie have you refused to confront? The greater the lie; the greater the emotional pain. If you confront every lie, it will reveal a truth. Remember, you shall know the truth, and the truth shall set you free.

The power of your purpose – keep it centre stage

William Barclay said, "There are two great days in a person's life - the day we are born and the day we discover why." The discovery of the "why" should become your passion and your desire. In the midst of adversity, your purpose in life will call you back into alignment. No matter what occurs, keep moving forward with your purpose in mind.

You must challenge your negative emotions in light of your purpose. One of the exercises in the workbook is to take a piece of paper and draw a line down the centre. On one side, make a note of your purpose and on the other, make a list of your daily activities and emotions.

Ask yourself "are my activities and emotions reconciling to my purpose?" If the answer is no, then you have to take massive intelligent and deliberate action. This starts with incremental steps to realign what you feel and what your activities are, to your purpose. One of the reasons why we get so easily side-tracked in our emotion, is because we are not taking any action to fulfil our purpose.

When purpose becomes the dominant force in your life, you will find a way to get back on track no matter what comes your way.

When I had purposed to run my own business, my daily activities included being sad, unhealthy eating, watching TV, thinking about the business but not taking any action towards it. You can see that there is a mismatch between what I purposed and my emotions and activities. I had to start realigning my activities and emotions with my purpose.

I looked at some quick wins, such as to decide a name for the company and register it. I replaced TV with motivational CDs, so that I could hear encouraging speakers that aligned with my purpose.

In the same way, if you want to feel joy and not sadness, then you have to do the things that will move you towards the joy you want to experience. This is a big part of my one-on-one coaching program. You have to take 100% responsibility for your current state. There are no short cuts.

Where you are now is as a direct result of your past thoughts and actions. If you don't want to replicate it in the future, you must change. What you will be tomorrow is a direct result of what you think and do today. If you are destiny minded, then you must reposition your thoughts and actions to line up with where you want to go and what you want to be.

Maintain a positive self-image

In simple terms, self-image is the image you have of yourself. It is not about being slim and attractive; I am not knocking it, self-image is about the self-worth and value that you put on your existence here in the world. You may be one of many on the earth, but your existence is still valuable. If you were not here, this world would have lost something, just ask someone you love or who loves you.

You are not nominal; you are phenomenal. You are not ordinary; you are extra-ordinary. There is no one else with your laughter, diction, eyes, DNA, thumbprint, shape, voice tonality, etc. They are all unique to you. Yes, you are one of a kind, a masterpiece, an original, so don't die a cheap copy.

How do you see yourself? When you think of the person you want to become, how do you think that person would behave in light of the problems, pain and crisis you have had? How do you think that person would adjust the image of himself or herself to come out on top as a positive unstoppable person, full of power? This is the kind of self-image you must start to build right now.

The lesson from the Rolls Royce owner

Have you heard the story of the man who owned a Rolls Royce? When asked if his Rolls Royce had broken down, he replied "Rolls Royce's never break down, mine just hesitates in going forward." That's the image of a Roll Royce. What is your image of yourself?

You may have broken down, but anything that is broken can be mended again, as long as it's not Humpty Dumpty. You must believe in yourself, if you don't, who will believe in you? Because you had an accident en route, doesn't mean you give up on your journey.

You should get up and get back on track and head towards your destination. The race is not for the swift or the strong but for those who endure to the very end[xvii]. It's never too late to turn things around.

Be mindful of the stories you tell yourself as to why you can't make it. New choices will give new results so you need to run that positive self- image in your head and commit it to paper. The following should help you build a good self-image:

- Create an inventory of who you are.
- List everything positive that you have accomplished in life.
- Develop a reading and listening plan of success stories and inspirational CDs to address your self-image.

- Make a list of the qualities you would like to have and start to use those qualities in your everyday life.
- Start to smile more and compliment others. Smiling release chemicals in the body, which helps with general well being according to Scientists.
- Build up your self-image by being of assistance to others and by finding ways to serve.

Don't live in the realm of what is; instead live in the realm of what can be. The quality of your self-image and the language you use around your image affects the quality of your life. No more effort is required to think good of yourself than to think badly. So, maximise your effort, go ahead and think good thoughts about yourself.

You must manage your emotion so that you can accomplish your future desires free from past hurts, stress, and depression. To do this you must plan. If you fail to plan, you plan to fail.

Points to ponder and act upon before you leave this section.

1. *What negative emotions do have every day?*

   ---

2. *What truth will you use to confront your negative emotions?*

   ---

3. *What positive emotions do you desire?*

   ---

4. *What action will you take every day to exhibit the emotions you desire?*

   ---

5. *Has someone hurt you who you need to forgive? What will you do?*

   ---

6. Write six things you will do to work on your self-image.

CHAPTER SEVEN
3-2-1 and Action

The reasonable man adapts himself to the world; the unreasonable one persists in trying to adapt the world to himself. Therefore, all progress depends on the unreasonable man.
-George Bernard Shaw

You have to pay the price to win the prize. -Rose Chandler.

Faith without works is dead

My Pastor reminded me that one action is better than 1000 good intentions. Everything that you have read in this book, up to now, will be wasted until you act. The power to change is not in what you read, but what you do. How much do you want to succeed? Are you willing to pay the price to win the prize? Will you maintain your status quo?

These are questions you must answer to get leverage on yourself to change. Your answer will determine the action you take. If you do nothing, you will remain stuck in a rut, but if you do something, you will become what you have never been before.

Action always speaks louder than words, because it demonstrates your desire for progress and achievement.

If you choose to remain the same, you have delegated your personal power to the people or the circumstance, which caused your pain. In many instances, the person has moved on or the circumstance has run its course, but you continue to exist but not live your life to the fullest.

Now your time has come. It's time to break through the pain of the past and plan the life you want for the future. I would encourage you to invest in the workbook and use it as a journal to track your personal journey to freedom. It goes into greater depth than the "points to ponder" at the end of each section of this book. It will be a memorabilia you will treasure and even pass on to the next generation.

It is not just your time, but it's also your turn. When it's time for an airplane to land, sometimes it has to circle overhead waiting for its turn. You have been going around in circles for too long; your time has come and now is your turn. The waiting is over. It's time to turn negativity to positivity, turn tears to joy, and turn your pain to power.

Turn means that which was concealed will now be revealed. You may have been sad, but your joy is about to be revealed; you may have been weak, but your strength is about to be revealed; you may have suffered much personal pain, but your power is about to be revealed.

I challenge you to take the eight day test based on the first eight chapters of this book. Take the time to think about and document your answers to every question asked in this book. Apply the strategies and techniques and see what will happen to you eight days from now. Eight in numerology signifies new beginnings. Eight days from today, when people meet you, they will encounter a new you, a better you, a joyful you, a more powerful you. Alternatively, you can book a one-to-one coaching session with me as we work through each chapter at a deeper level. Further information is available at the end of this book.

Become unreasonable with yourself about making a change and set out to persist until you achieve it. To turn your life around will not happen by osmosis but by taking consistent and persistent action towards your desired purpose.

So let's consider the actions you should take:

Massive Intelligent and Deliberate Actions (M.I.D.A.s™)

You don't just want to take action; you want to take intelligent and deliberate action to move you from where you are to where you want to be. I call it the M.I.D.A.s™ touch. Having travelled this far you should begin to develop your M.I.D.A.s™ to address the following areas in your life:

1. What do you want to achieve or become?

Bronnie Ware, an Australian nurse, spent several years at work in palliative care. Bronnie said the number-one regret of the dying was that they wished they had the courage to live life true to themselves, and not a life that others expected of them. Imagine what it would be like to look back over your life with that regret. You should make up your mind today that you will become everything you know you were born to be.

No one knows the length of their years on earth. Therefore, isn't it time you plan your dream and live your dream? The plan for your life must start with your purpose.

If you are unsure about what you want to accomplish in life, you can start to ask yourself a few questions and see what comes to your mind:

- What do you most enjoy doing?
- If you would have a role, what would it be?
- What are you happiest doing?
- What is the one thing that when you do it makes you feel alive?
- If you had all the money in the world, what would you do with your time?

Everyone is extremely good at something, so it is your responsibility to find out what yours is and put your whole self into it without any reservations. This is the thing you were born to do.

You should also think about and plan your personal and professional goals in life:

Personal goals might include:

- Health, exercise, character traits, spirituality, family, emotions, beliefs, mind-set, personal net worth, etc.

Professional goals might include:

- Income, qualifications, investments, business, career, growth, knowledge, networks, business net worth, etc.

When you do this kind of brainstorming, you can end up with a long list of items. The key is to prioritise the ones that are most closely aligned to your purpose and plan to do these first. So for example, if your purpose in life is to be a public speaker, this can be taxing on the body so you might set yourself a health goal and network goal as a priority over the others.

2. Document your dream/goal/objective

You should take a long-term view of your future and commit your dreams to paper. Write the vision and make it plain, so that when you read it you can run your life by it.[xviii]

The M.I.D.A.s™ for your life will be effective if you set yourself SMART goals:

- **S**pecific means simple but it stretches you
- **M**easurable means it is manageable and meaningful
- **A**chievable means it is ambitious and attainable
- **R**elevant means it is realistic and result focused
- **T**imely mean it is traceable and time bound

Document your goals in the positive and focus on what you want, i.e. what you want to gain and not what you want to lose. A positive statement is more empowering than a negative one. For example "my goal is to be financially independent" rather than "I want to be debt free." Or, "my goal is to be at my ideal weight," rather than "I want to lose 10 lbs."

The focus should be on what you want to gain, have or achieve, not what you will lose. So write your desired outcome in the positive to empower you to achieve it. This must be crystal clear to you because it will become the focus of your attention. It must be in positive language because where your attention goes, creativity flows, and this means you will be flooded with new ideas about how to make your dream a reality, because you will attract whatever you think about.

3. Why do you desire it?

You need an empowering reason why you want to achieve what you want to achieve. So, if it's your ideal weight:

- Is it to have more energy to accomplish your life purpose?
- To play fully with the children and give them the quality time and fun they desire?
- To live longer and reduce the risk of health issues in later life?

What is your "why"? The longer your list of why, the more likely you are to accomplish your desire. Try to write at least 20 reasons why you must accomplish your desire/ objective/goal. Bill Walsh says, "If your why is strong enough, you'll figure out the how."

4. What values are you willing to live your life by to accomplish your dream?

Write your top five values, the most important first. For example, will it be family, honesty, integrity, success, respect, flexibility, self-discipline, and freedom. The values determine what is important to you, as you pursue your dream. So if you want to be healthy for your family, you will not pursue wealth and success at the risk to your health. Your values set the code of your personal conduct, which determines what you believe in and stand for.

Big on my values list is self-discipline. This gives me the ability to determine my response to any given situation. Self-discipline is synonymous with a sound mind. A sound mind is rational, measured and a reasoned mind. When you have self-discipline, you will evaluate the options, and then you'll act and not react. Your values will help to shape your personality and character in life, so consider them carefully in light of what you want to become or achieve. As a man thinks in his heart, so is he.

5. Get leverage on yourself

You have the master key to unlock everything that has held you back. If you are not achieving your dream, then you will need a check-up because something has stopped you in your tracks and impeded your progress. If it's your thoughts, you should challenge any stinking thinking with logic and reason, and be true to yourself. If you look for the truth, you will find it.

If it's your belief system, then you should work through and challenge your beliefs. Re-read the sections on "I was just thinking" and "I believe," and focus, analyse and address your issues in light of the stories mentioned. What lie has been hidden in the dark that you need to expose to the light?

Here are some of the beliefs that prevent people from being successful:

- I don't have what it takes.
- I don't have the time.
- What if people reject me?
- I am afraid.

Here are some of the beliefs of successful people:

- All skills are learnable.
- Anything is possible.
- The only failure is not to try.
- People make time for what is important to them.
- I have a desire to succeed.
- Rejection will give me direction.

Wrong and negative beliefs must be challenged and replaced with positive and empowering beliefs that serve your purpose and your goals.

Have your emotions tied you up? Half the battle is won if you address your thoughts and beliefs. Begin to list and be aware of the negative emotions that have held you back. Is it anger, depression, rejection? You have to plan to replace these emotions with what you desire, such as peace, joy and acceptance. You should measure and score yourself on a scale of 1 to 10 daily, and verify that you are moving away from the negative towards the positive emotions.

More on this is provided within the workbook if your wish to delve deeper into this issue. To transition from pain to power, you should plan to:

- Forgive.
- Expose lies to the truth.
- Know your purpose and live on purpose.
- Improve your self-image.

For every other reason you have noted, you must demolish the legs that have supported the lie with the truth, and identify new beliefs, new empowering stories with endless possibilities.

When I was made redundant, I told myself that I would never work again. I had to get to a place where I challenged my own thoughts, which lead me to document my skills, knowledge, expertise and life experiences to demolish the legs off the lies I had told myself, and replace them with empowering truths.

Had I not challenged my assertions, I would not have had the courage to start my own consulting business. You must also plan to challenge everything that has held you back. This can also be achieved by positive incantations.

6. Connectivity for accountability

It is good to connect with like-minded people or an individual who can hold you accountable for your progress. Better still, both of you can walk through the process and hold each other accountable.

You need to find someone who is on your wavelength. Someone you can trust and rely on, and who wants the best for you. Confide in that person and ask them to hold you accountable for the actions you take which are in harmony and which are not in harmony with your goals in life. They are there to ensure you keep on track. If you can teach what you have learnt from this book to each other, then you can live it.

In addition, whatever you want to achieve, find the experts who have already achieved it, and invest in their knowledge through the purchase of their CDs and attendance at their seminars or webinars. Success leaves clues and speeds up your progress, so don't reinvent what has already been invented, just model it and use it to your benefit. It's time to switch off the TV and be proactive in living a fulfilled life.

What actions will you take in the short, medium and long term to accomplish your dream?

80% of your results will come from 20% of your actions. The fact that you have a written M.I.D.A.s™ means you have increased the likelihood that you will achieve your goals by 1000%

Identify the actions you plan to take today, next week, next month, etc., which will move you towards your goal.

7. Plan to get physical and nutritional

When I decided to set up my business, I realised I had gotten out of balance. Scientists have said that physiology changes psychology. When you think positive thoughts and move your body at the same time, it changes significantly how you feel.

Have you ever seen someone jogging who also looked depressed as the same time? No, nor have I. What you do with your physical body will enhance the speed of change, whilst you transition from pain to power.

Before you embark on any change like this, you should seek medical advice. Do something physical like jogging. If you don't like the outdoors, you can do a workout at home. If you are not the workout type, you could try an exercise ball or a rebounder. If you don't like that, try jogging on the spot for 5-15 minutes, or if you are concerned about the noise, you can walk on the spot for 5-15 minutes. If all else fails, you can put on your favourite music and dance for a few minutes. Now you have no excuse for not being active.

Get your body on the move, do something with it and produce some energy. You will be shocked at how much better you will feel and how much better you will sleep. Be inspired about the person you are becoming.

To complement the new you and your new regime, you should also watch what you eat. Try to introduce some live foods into your diet. By live, I mean fresh fruits and vegetables, and eat some raw foods too. Monitor and record how you feel daily, now that you have made some better choices about your life.

Below I have included an extract of what your M.I.D.A.s™ for a particular goal might look like. This is the same principle for short, medium or long terms goals and objectives, or your dream.

Ralph Waldo Emerson said, "That which we persist in doing becomes easier for us to do, not that the nature of the thing itself is changed, but our power to do it is increased."

You can find these Biblical secrets in the book of Nehemiah in the Bible. It is an interesting read. You will find many Biblical principles in this book from the life of Nehemiah who had a goal to rebuild the broken down walls of Jerusalem within 52 days. You will find that the challenges he faced then, are the same ones we are facing today; but he overcame them and accomplished his goal. You can too.

In closing this chapter I would encourage you to place your goal in your bedroom, on your phone, or somewhere where you can see and read it at least three times per day. Read it out aloud. This acts as a powerful reminder of what you plan to achieve and where you are heading.

Points to ponder and act upon before you leave this section

Example M.I.D.A.s™ of one priority goal, which contributes towards the main purpose.

Massive Intelligent and Deliberate Actions (M.I.D.A.s™)			
Life Purpose: *To be a public speaker who transform minds so people can live a fulfilled live*			
Values are: self discipline, family, honesty & integrity			
Name: Susie Brown			**Date:** 2 July 2013
Personal Goal Title: Health			**Accountable to:** Jan Berg (friend)
SMART Goal 1: To achieve my ideal weight of 70kg by xyz.			
Why (reasons) • To have energy to deliver an inspiring message on stage and be helpful to others. • To play with my children without running out of energy. • For my future health and well being.			
Barriers (want to move away from) • I cook quick snacks and junk food for the family all the time. • I comfort eat when I am alone. • I love chocolate.		**Empowering (want to move towards)** • I choose to cook healthy meals for myself and my family. • I will be productive around the house when I am alone. • I choose to eat healthy snacks or fruit instead.	
Today:	Daily:	Weekly:	Monthly:
Engage support of family.	Read my M.I.D.A.s™ morning, noon and night.	Dance to favorite music for 5-15 minutes twice per week.	Reward self for achievement by going to the spa.
Plan meals and shopping ahead.	Measure my mood on a scale of 1-10.	Go for a walk and enjoy nature once per week.	If I have had a relapse I will not give up but persevere.
Document only what I will eat and drink.	Eat and drink what I have prepared.	Weigh myself and record progress.	
	Replace chocolate with fruit.	Maintain self-discipline towards my goal.	
	Read my "I am" statements.		

The M.I.D.A.s™ can be used for any areas of your life and to accomplish any short, medium or long term goal. The benefit of the M.I.D.A.s™ is that it allows you to see the connections between your purpose, the values you have, your SMART goals, why you must achieve them, what the barriers are, how you plan to overcome them, and the actions you will take daily, weekly and monthly towards your achievement. It all flows together and gives visibility of what you plan to do and why. This is more inspiring than a long "to-do list."

So you can use the M.I.D.A.s™ to turnaround your life. "If you plan it and take action, you will achieve it." Rose Chandler.

Having done all this, what should this new turnaround, powerful person look like? Let's have a look.

Section Three:
The turnaround you.
Who are you now?

CHAPTER EIGHT

The New You

Although no one can go back and make a brand-new start, anyone can start from now and make a brand-new ending. -Carl Bard

Be ye transformed by the renewing of your mind. -Romans 12: 2

Live your life with meaning

When you have a purpose in life, you will overcome obstacles and wake up each morning with a new zest for live. The new you is the positive you who sees things from a different perspective and understands that it will work out in your favour. You have come full circle to release that the power lies within, and that when you exercise your power, you are unstoppable.

Be clear about who you are – clarity is power. When challenges come your way in the future, remind your challenges who you are, you are the boss! This is what you have accomplished on your journey, and I call these reminders the "I am statements." You should read them aloud every day with all the emotions and meaning you can muster.

In reality, the more you hear them, the more faith arises in you about who you are:

- I am courageous.
- I am a possibility thinker.
- I am an overcomer.
- I am forgiven.
- I am love.
- I am persistent.
- I am joyful.

- I am determined.
- I am prosperous.
- I am positive.
- I am rich in thought and deed.
- I am a blessing to others.
- I am blessed.
- I am unstoppable.
- I am changing for the better each and every day.
- I am free from the past.
- I am healed.
- I am strong.
- I am successful.
- I am more than a conqueror.
- I am powerful.
- I am balanced in body, soul and spirit.
- I am a creative teacher that touches lives.
- I am an inspirational role model that changes lives.
- I am an outstanding leader that defies the odds.
- I am a fearless champion who lives life to the full.
- I am a confident achiever who makes a difference.

Yes, you are all that and so much more. You have done what others thought about but refused to do. You have regained your personal power, and from this day you will never again hand it over voluntarily or by force to anyone or any circumstance. Your power is in you and no one can take it from you.

Don't leave home without your "I am statements". You will need them to face the challenges of the day as you recap on each statement. Put them in your phone and read them throughout the day and last thing at night. These statements will reinforce and strengthen your inner being, and your subconscious mind every day. Anytime a challenge arises, your subconscious mind will pull out an "I am statement" to counter any negative emotional response. You will be lifted with resolve as you say, "I am more than enough for this adversity." Speak out aloud who you are and let adversity and crisis know that from now on you are a force to be reckoned with.

Next to the Bible, the two books that influence my life are *Think and Grow Rich* by Napoleon Hill, and *Awaken the Giant Within* by Tony Robbins. Both books advocate that you repeat, that which empowers you, on a daily basis. Your future greatness is based on the small things you do each day, so don't neglect the small and the repetitive activities.

Program your new mindset for success

You will become what you think. Commit daily to think about your thoughts based on what you feel. If you feel sad, then do that check-up from the neck up. Switch your thoughts and focus to the positive and not the negative. Of course, negative thoughts will come, but you have the power not to allow them to dominate and rule your day or your life.

Remember you have to move from a place of pain to a place of power by your thoughts. What you think about and give your focus to, you will attract.

Napoleon Hill reminds us that thoughts are things. Your thoughts and feelings will create your life, so think good thoughts, and you will experience good emotions, and good things will come to your life.

Visualize the person you want to become. Visualise the result, and see yourself in your mind as if you were that person right now. What you think is what you will become.

Henry Ford said, "To see a thing clearly in the mind makes it begin to take form." Can you see the new turnaround you in action? That is the person you should be every single day.

"Watch your thoughts, they become your actions; watch your actions, they become your habits; watch your habits, they become your character; watch your character, it becomes your destiny." – Frank Outlaw

Track your daily emotions

Every single day, determine what emotions you want to feel or create in your life. These could be peace, joy, gratitude, contentment, excitement, euphoria, passion, surprise, happiness. The new you will no longer be stuck in self-pity or pain, but will have crafted the positive emotions that you desire and want. Your challenge - how far on the scale from 1 to 10 will you score yourself for positive emotions each day?

Know your empowering beliefs

The new you has displaced and moved away from every negative belief that has restricted you or held you back. Positive beliefs focus on possibility, limitless opportunities, gratitude and anything that empowers you to become more today that you were yesterday. The new you have removed your limitations.

You and your body

Money can buy you healing but not health. Your health is so valuable, that you must keep it in its optimal state. Your optimal physical new regime should address the mental, spiritual, physical and nutritional. You are what you eat, and so the new you should address both the psychological and the physical. Someone said "I pray to keep my spirit active, I read to keep my mind alert and I exercise and eat right to keep my body in shape."

Remain inspired

The new you can always ask an empowering question like:

- What can I do to help?
- How can I add value to this situation right now?
- What can I do to turn this around?
- What is the solution to this problem?

The new you is the empowered you, the one who takes 100% responsibility for your actions. From this moment forward, you know that test will come, but the new you is now equipped with strategies and tactics that have been successfully used to address the past and keep moving forward, even if you became a moulting eagle – it is only for a season and you will bounce back stronger and better than before.

I heard someone say that the cheetah made it to the ark and so did the snail. The race is neither for the swift nor the strong, but for those who endure to the very end, so endure what you have to, but keep the movement forward. Whenever you recognise old patterns trying to make a re-entry into your life, you know how to deal with them by doing what you know is right.

What will you do with the remaining time you have on the earth?

Be determined that when you die, people will know that you have lived. William Shakespeare reminded us that all the world is a stage, and we are merely players; we have our exits and entrances and one man in his time plays many parts.

The question is, will you play your part and be your part? You were made on purpose with a purpose to fulfil in your lifetime. The new you is active, everyday living your purpose and having a fulfilled life. The new you has learnt the lessons from the past and use them to empower your future, so that you live a life of self-mastery; not misery.

The new you will be it, do it, love it and live it.

Points to ponder and act upon before you leave this section.

1. What meaning have you given to your life? Document your purpose.

   ----

2. Document five "I am statements" which line up to you purpose.

   ----

3. What three positive things you will meditate on each day about your purpose?

   ----

4. What emotions will you exhibit each day towards your purpose?

   ----

5. What are your three main beliefs about your purpose?

   ----

6. How do you plan to take care of your body, soul and spirit?

   ----

7. What empowering question will you ask in any negative situation?

   ----

8. What will you do with the remainder of your time on earth?

CHAPTER: NINE

"D.E.S.I.R.E."™ The Formula

Dream no small dreams for they have no power to move the hearts of men. -Johann Wolfgang von Goethe.

He who has a why to live for can bear almost any how.-Nietzsche.

Discover the keys

We have seen people from all walks of life who repositioned themselves and gathered momentum to live a fulfilling life. It is like they have shed the old self and took on a new identity. In reality, what has happened is that the baggage of the old emotional burdens has been lifted and a new release of life has begun. Maybe you just want greater focus to live a more fulfilled life, but don't know where to start and what to do. I have created the life-changing D.E.S.I.R.E.™ formula for you to develop and live the life you have always wanted.

The secret D.E.S.I.R.E.™ formula has the following functions:

Dream: what it is that you want to accomplish, what is your dream, your goal in life, what are you inspired to do or become? Commit your dream to paper.

Envision: can you visualise it in your mind? Put yourself in the picture and see yourself fulfilling your dream now. See the person you will become and your characteristics on display. Picture how you will talk, walk, dress, behave. Picture everything about your dream before it happens. Make the picture come alive in your mind; this is your cinematic preview of your forthcoming attraction.

Specific: have a specific Massive Intelligent and Deliberate Actions (M.I.D.A.s™) about what you will do, by when, and most importantly, why you will do it. Plan it, but most important of all, do it. If you fail to plan you have planned to fail.

Inspect: you must inspect what you expect. You cannot control what you refuse to measure, so you must monitor your M.I.D.A.s™ to see if you are getting the desired results or not.

Revise: If you are not getting the desired result, you can either revise the actions you plan to take or make your goals more realistic for you to achieve. The objective behind the revision is that your actions are aligned, and achieving your goal.

Energise: you need energy for where you are going. You should plan to address the "T.E.E.N"™ as you transition to live a fulfilled live.

- **T**houghts - be positive
- **E**motions - let go of the past, forgive quickly and move forward
- **E**xercise - to energise your body for peak performance
- **N**utrition - to feed your body and keep it healthy

You are worth the effort, the time and the investment. Take the time and go through the process of turning misery to mastery, pain into power and live a fulfilled life. This is the formula for you to dream and live a fulfilling life.

You can only live the life of your dreams, not by accident but by design.

-Rose Chandler

To your success! Design your Life

Be it. Do it. Love it. Live it.

Feedback:

If you have read this book, I would love to know if it made a difference to your life. Please drop me a line with your feedback and comments to:

info@RoseChandler.co.uk   or   info@PainToPower.co.uk

Coaching Service:

Special accelerated 1 on 1 coaching discount is available for those who have purchased this book.

From ~~$97~~ to $67 per week for my 8 weeks Pain to Power Accelerated Turnaround Coaching program. Use the $67 coupon below to get your first week free when you sign up. This is a one-on-one coaching program with me on SKYPE.

What you will get. I will show you how to:

- ✓ Identify why you have become stuck and start to turn your life around
- ✓ Identify and deal with what is making you angry and depressed
- ✓ Break through limiting beliefs to access your future
- ✓ Learn how to completely and totally forgive
- ✓ Identify you purpose in life
- ✓ Develop empowering "I am Statements" to propel you into your future
- ✓ Turn your mood around at the click of a finger
- ✓ Program your mind for daily success
- ✓ Breakthrough the intensity of negative emotions and feel energized
- ✓ Develop you own personal M.I.D.A.s™ for the achievement of your goals and monitor your progress
- ✓ Turnaround difficult relationships, be it at home or at work

- ✓ Have a better relationship with the people around you
- ✓ Build confidence and self-esteem to propel you into your future
- ✓ Develop unstoppable momentum to achieve your goals in life
- ✓ Use the D.E.S.I.R.E^{TM} formula to design and live your dream.

For more information visit http://RoseChandler.co.uk.

It you want to turn your life around - it starts with a decision.

Decisions decide destiny: Tony Robbins

There is a money back guarantee on this offer.

Follow me on Social media:

 https://twitter.com/RoseMChandler

 https://www.facebook.com/RoseChandlerAuthorSpeaker

Websites:

http://RoseChandler.co.uk

http://PainToPower.co.uk

Emails:

info@RoseChandler.co.uk

info@PainToPower.co.uk

Biz@PainToPower.co.uk

Telephone:

Tel + 44 (0) 7525 348 007

New Products

Sign up for new products via email at Biz@PaintoPower.co.uk on the Turnaround series:

- Pain to Power Workbook
- Pain to Power Home Study Kit
- Pain to Power Inspiration cards
- Pain to Power Audio book

$67.00
Coupon

**Redeemable against
the purchase**

of

Your 8 weeks Pain to Power
one-on-one
coaching program

Bibliography

Bible End Notes

i Mark 10:51

ii John 8:32

iii Ephesians4:26

iv Proverbs 20:5

v John 4:

vi Joshua 2:1-21; 6:17,22,23,25 and Matthew 1:5; Hebrew 11:3; James 2:25

vii 1 Thessalonians 4:13-14

viii Philippians 4:8

ix 1 Samuel 30:6

x Proverbs 25:28

xi John 8:32

xii 2 Corinthians 4:16

xiii Isaiah 40:31

xiv 1 Corinthians 2:8

xv Philippians 3:13

xvi Matthew 5:43-48

xvii Ecclesiastes 9:11

xviii Habakkuk 2:2

www.ingramcontent.com/pod-product-compliance
Lightning Source LLC
Chambersburg PA
CBHW061658040426
42446CB00010B/1803